If you're someone who finds yourself asking, "Is this all there is?" . . . someone who wonders why you have everyone else's dream life and want out, or someone who's so damn tired of waiting to earn the right to be yourself, this book is for you. When you've "done everything" and wonder why it's not enough, Kim has the answer. Not just why you feel that way, but what's missing, and how to fix it once and for all. Inducing out loud laughs, tears of recognition, and a feeling of being seen, Kim gives the high achievers of the world the answers they've been seeking for a lifetime.

**April Shprintz, Business Accelerator,
Creator of The Generosity Culture® and
Award-Winning Author of *Magic Blue Rocks:
The Secret To Doing Anything***

Strategic Unruliness is the GPS for transformation. Kim's clear, engaging storytelling outlines how to get to the heart of what matters most—YOUR way. Decades of conditioning dissolve, empowering you to elevate your innate talents and gifts without hesitation or apology. A must-read for any leader who landed at their desk on a Monday, wondering, "Is this it?"

Tracey Selingo, Founder, Fork Over Love

STRATEGIC UNRULINESS

Break the Rules.
BUILD WHAT'S NEXT.

KIM BOLOURTCHI

STRATEGIC UNRULINESS
Break the Rules. Build What's Next.
Kim Bolourtchi

Published by The Northlight Press, St. Louis, MO
Copyright ©2025 Kim Bolourtchi
All rights reserved.

No part of this publication may be reproduced, stored in a retrieval system, or transmitted in any form or by any means, electronic, mechanical, photocopying, recording, scanning, or otherwise, except as permitted under Section 107 or 108 of the 1976 United States Copyright Act, without the prior written permission of the Publisher. Requests to the Publisher for permission should be addressed to the Permissions Department, the Northlight Press, and info@kimbolourtchi.com.

Project Management and Book Design: DavisCreativePublishing.com
Cover Design: Missy Asikainen
Editor: Sandra Matteucci

Library of Congress Cataloging-in-Publication Data
Names: Bolourtchi, Kim, author.
Title: Strategic unruliness : break the rules, build what's next / Kim Bolourtchi.
Description: St Louis, MO : The Northlight Press, [2025]
Identifiers: LCCN: 2025918152 | ISBN: 9781732902411 (paperback) | 9781732902435 (hardback) | 9781732902428 (ebook)
Subjects: LCSH: Leadership. | Success in business. | Motivation (Psychology) | Assertiveness (Psychology) | BISAC: BUSINESS & ECONOMICS / Leadership. | BUSINESS & ECONOMICS / Motivational. | SELF-HELP / Personal Growth / Success.
Classification: LCC: HD57.7 .B65 2025 | DDC: 658.4092--dc23

ATTENTION CORPORATIONS, UNIVERSITIES, COLLEGES, AND PROFESSIONAL ORGANIZATIONS: Quantity discounts are available on bulk purchases of this book for educational, gift or special event purposes. For information, please contact Kim Bolourtchi, The Northlight Press Company, info@kimbolourtchi.com.

For Ray, Sam, and Nick—

*Thank you for always seeing me,
for trusting me to model a way of being that has
no roadmap, and for living Strategic Unruliness™
with fearless conviction—before there was proof it worked.*

I love you endlessly.

YOU ALREADY KNOW

You are successful on the outside.
But something's off. This book names what you've been
carrying and dares you to lead from the truth.

Table of Contents

Foreword ix
Preface xiii
Author's Note xv
Introduction: This Is Not Another Leadership Book xix

PART I: THE UNRAVELING

Chapter One: Exposed 1
A glitter bomb in court. Public exposure becomes personal liberation.

Chapter Two: The Rules That Raised You 13
You didn't choose these rules. But they still run you. Let's name them

Chapter Three: The Hidden Cost of Obedience 21
Being good means being small. This chapter is the receipt.

Chapter Four: Unraveling in Real Time 29
Don't wait for the rebrand. The real work starts in the free fall.

PART II: THE RECKONING

Chapter Five: Say the Thing 41
No more filtering. Say the truth that changes everything.

Chapter Six: Say the Fucking Thing (Even on LinkedIn) 51
Authentic voice over algorithm. This is what happens when you lead unfiltered.

Chapter Seven: Limits and Leverage 57
Your constraints are trying to tell you something. Listen.

Chapter Eight: The Day That Shifted Everything 67
Clarity hits like lightning. Disorienting. Electric. True.

PART III: THE REBUILD

Chapter Nine: The Power of Integration 75
You're not too much. You're divided. This chapter brings you home.
Chapter Ten: Power That Starts in Your Feet 77
You can't lead from your head alone. Get in your body. Ground your power.

Chapter Eleven: Leading Without Applause 87
There won't be claps. Just your clarity and conviction. Lead anyway.

Chapter Twelve: When Pushback Means You're Close 95
Resistance isn't rejection. It's proof you're on the edge of something real.

Chapter Thirteen: Live Unruly 107
Not a concept. A way of being. Rituals. Non-negotiables. Realness.

Chapter Fourteen: Build What's Next 117
You didn't come this far to replicate a system. You came to create.

Epilogue: So, What Now? 135
Afterword 139

Foreword

I need to tell you something right up front: I wasn't supposed to write this foreword.

Not because I'm unqualified—I've spent my entire career studying what it takes to create cultures worth fighting for, and I've written three books on how we can lead with kindness, civility, and authenticity. But when Kim asked me to write this, my first instinct was to say no because I knew exactly what she was asking me to do: to stand beside someone who refuses to follow the rules that keep the rest of us comfortable and safe.

And as a lifelong (and recovering) rule-follower, that terrified me.

In full transparency, I've built my career on being a proud Kindness Extremist—teaching people how to actively lead with kindness while maintaining their careers, their credibility, and their most meaningful relationships. I've shown thousands of people how to be authentically vulnerable without being seen as weak, how to challenge dysfunction without burning bridges, how to lead with heart while keeping their backbone intact.

But Kim? Kim is asking for something different entirely.

She's not asking you to merely be a good human while you navigate the system. She's asking you to question whether the system deserves your compliance in the first place.

When I first read this manuscript, I felt that familiar tightness in my chest, the same feeling I get when someone is about to do something that makes me think, *"Oh no, they're going too far."* Because that's what Kim does. She goes to places that many believe are too far. She dances on keynote stages when the industry says that's "unprofessional." She'll drop an F-bomb on LinkedIn when the algorithm punishes authenticity. She wears the catsuit when everyone else is in sequins, and she wins anyway.

And here's the best part about this: She's right.

She's right that most of us are performing a version of leadership that was never designed for our full selves. She's right that the rules we follow to stay "acceptable" are the same rules that keep us small. She's right that somewhere along the way, we traded our fire for approval and called it wisdom.

I know this because I've seen it in my own life. For years, I told the story of my suicide attempt—the darkest moment when workplace bullying nearly broke me—because I knew it would help others. But I also softened it. Made it palatable. Wrapped it in lessons and takeaways so people wouldn't have to sit with the raw reality of what it actually feels like to be so broken by work that you want to die.

Kim doesn't soften anything.

She describes standing in a courthouse bathroom, dissociating in real time—the inevitable result of splitting yourself in half just to belong. She talks about finding the courage to dismiss judgmental glances from friends and family, to stop hiding her love of dance and, more fundamentally, to stop hiding who she truly is. Above all, she makes clear that the path of Strategic Unruliness™ isn't easy, but she renders its benefits impossible to ignore.

And that's exactly what we need right now.

I've learned a lot from working with thousands of leaders, but here's the most powerful lesson: The leaders who change everything aren't the ones who follow the playbook. They're the ones who have the audacity to believe that their way of leading unapologetically —and, with kindness and self-awareness—might actually be what the world is waiting for.

Kim's framework—Get Radically Clear, Find Your Limits, Challenge the Rules, Expand Capacity—isn't just about personal transformation. It's about cultural revolution. Every time one person stops shrinking to fit the room, they expand what's possible for everyone else in that space.

I've witnessed this firsthand. I've watched leaders who thought they had to choose between being liked and being respected discover that respect actually comes from being courageously kind and authentic. I've seen teams transform when their leader stopped managing perception and started leading from truth. I've watched cultures shift when someone had the guts to say, *"This rule doesn't serve us anymore. What if we tried something different?"*

That's what Strategic Unruliness™ makes possible. Not chaos. Not rebellion for its own sake. But clarity—the radical kind. The kind that separates the signal from the noise, names what's not working, and builds something better from the ground up.

Will it be comfortable? Absolutely not. Will some people resist? Count on it. Will you question yourself a thousand times? Probably. But will you finally feel like you're leading from the center of who you actually are instead of the edges of who you think you should be?

Yes.

And that's everything.

We need people who will dance on the keynote stage, not because it's strategic, but because that's what integrity looks like when it refuses to apologize for taking up space.

We need people who will say the thing that makes the room uncomfortable, not because they want to shock, but because truth has a way of cutting through performance and landing where it needs to land.

We need people who will choose alignment over approval, every single time, until alignment becomes the new standard.

That's what this book offers: not another leadership strategy you can implement without changing who you are, but an invitation to finally become who you've always been underneath all the editing.

The world doesn't need more leaders who know how to follow a script. It needs leaders who know themselves so deeply, trust themselves so completely, and commit to their vision so fiercely that they create new possibilities just by showing up fully.

Kim is one of those leaders. And after reading this book, you might discover you are too.

Let's find out what happens when you stop shrinking and start building.

The future is waiting. Let's get unruly.

Shola Richards
CEO and Founder, Go Together Global®
Author of *Making Work Work*, *Go Together*, and *Civil Unity*

PREFACE:
The Ache Is Universal

This book was born from my lived experience as a woman, a rule-follower, a high-performer who woke up in a life that looked perfect and felt wrong. So yes, some of these stories are about women. Because they're real. Because they're mine. Because they matter.

But don't mistake that for exclusivity.

The ache I write about—the pressure to perform, the fear of being too much, the hunger to lead from truth instead of optics—that's not gendered. That's human.

The leaders I work with are founders, CEOs, executives, and rising leaders who look like they have it all and secretly wonder why it still feels off. They come to me when success no longer fits. When the old rules stop working. When they're finally ready to build something honest.

So, ignore the boxes and labels; this book transcends them.

If you've ever felt the tension between who you are and who success told you to be . . .
If you've ever followed every rule and still felt fractured . . .
If you've ever wondered why a life that looks so good still feels so hollow,
You're in the right place.

This book is just the beginning.

If at any point you find yourself thinking, *I don't just want to read this, I want to live it,* I'd love to hear from you. Send me a note at kim@kimbolourtchi.com and tell me what stood out to you. I read every message, and your story matters to me.

AUTHOR'S NOTE:

Before the Clarity

The contradictions I carried before I broke the rules.

I was loved.
I was also abused.

I was captain of the Pom Squad and President of Student Council.
I was also the one not invited when friends had to choose just one.

I choreographed state-winning dance routines.
I also tried to end my life. To make someone notice.

I was told I was lucky to be adopted.
And constantly reminded I was second-class.

I was accused of killing Jesus in 7th grade.
And stunned to learn some people believed I had.

I drove my parents' car every weekend when I was 13.
I forced my little sister to lie on the floorboard so we wouldn't get caught.

I made choking sounds and grabbed my throat every time my mom lit a cigarette.
I also stole her Marlboro Lights and smoked them on the roof.

I stood up for others constantly.
And still wondered if anyone would stand for me.

I was told I was talented enough to be a national dance champion.
I just had to change how I danced. And how I looked.

I was asked to solve the problems in my family.
And criticized for being too bossy, too much.

I was praised for raising strong, independent kids.
But not for letting my daughter wear my son's shorts to school.

I was told my uniqueness was a superpower.
Just don't dance.

I had a secret fort in the woods called Terabithia.
I went there to read smut novels when I was eleven.

I nearly drowned in water I could stand in—twice.
I also rescued a dog from the ice when it fell through a lake.

I was three but told to lie and say I was two so I could fly for free.
Later, I got my mouth washed out with soap . . . for lying.

I twice signed six-figure contracts with less than $1,000 in my account.
Because I knew it would work out. And it did.

I was determined to be the best girl ever. To follow every rule.
And I swore I'd never submit.

Here's what I didn't know yet:
You can follow every rule and still feel fractured.
You can do everything "right" and still be punished.
You can win and still feel wrong.

Before the clarity came the chaos.
Before the clarity came the confusion.
Before the clarity, I thought *I* was the problem.

But I wasn't.

The problem was the invisible limits I didn't know I'd internalized.
The script I didn't write, but still followed.
The system that rewarded performance and punished wholeness.

This isn't only my story.
It's yours too if you've ever felt like you had to edit yourself to survive.
If you've ever contorted to fit what "success" demanded.
If you've ever had a moment when you thought: *I'm doing everything they told me to do, so why does it still feel off?*

This book is about the contradictions, the conditioning, the clarity, and the choice you now get to make:
To keep performing your life . . .
Or to embody it—fully, fiercely, and without apology.

To keep following scripts that keep you small . . .
Or to break them—strategically, deliberately, and with vision.

That's the choice.
And when you choose to lead Strategically Unruly™,
You don't just change yourself.
You change your team.
You change your organization.
You change your life.

INTRODUCTION:
This Is Not Another Leadership Book

What if the rules you've been following are the very thing holding you back?

There's a kind of success no one talks about.
The kind that looks brilliant from the outside—polished title, stacked resume, impressive results—but feels like a slow leak on the inside.

You're winning. But you're also withering.
And no one sees it but you.

You still show up. Still deliver. Still carry the room.
But under the surface? There's a question forming, one you're afraid to say out loud:

"Is this it?"

Maybe it's not burnout.
Maybe it's not boredom.

Maybe it's this:
No one sees the real me.

You mastered a role that was never really yours, and now it's too small to contain you.
Not because you failed. But because it was shaped by rules you didn't choose.

Rules about how to lead.
How to speak.
How to look.
How to perform being "enough."

And the cost of staying in character?
It's starting to feel unbearable.

Because if this is what success is supposed to feel like . . .

Why do you feel so restless?
Why are you so damn tired, not just in your body, but in your spirit?

Some feel it as restlessness. Others stifle quiet rage.
The gnawing sense that they've optimized everything except the part of them that actually wants to stay.

Why does the life that you painstakingly built sometimes feel like a performance you can't quit?

You're not crazy.
You're not broken.
And you're definitely not ungrateful.

You're waking up.

I've seen this ache show up in boardrooms and back offices, in the loudest voices and the quietest leaders.

Some talk about it. Some bury it.
But the tension is the same:

They're allowed to be bold but not vulnerable.
Decisive but not uncertain.
Praised for being unshakeable and punished the moment they show a crack.

So, they perform. They produce. They power through.
But underneath the surface, they ache.

That ache?
It's not burnout.

It's the early warning sign of misalignment.
The kind that slowly drains your energy, dulls your instincts, and distances you from the vision that once lit you up.

Not because you're failing.
But because you're trying to build the future while operating inside limits designed for the past.

Ignore it too long, and it starts showing up in real ways:
Stalled momentum.
Fractured team dynamics.
A creeping sense of mediocrity in work that used to feel meaningful.

It's not a mood. It's a signal. And it matters.

It's what tells you:
You've been living by rules you didn't write, and they won't get you where you're meant to go.

Strategic Unruliness™ is what happens when you stop shrinking to fit and start leading from the part of you that never asked for permission.

Not for shock value.
Not for rebellion's sake.

But because the system you've been succeeding in was never designed for your full power.

Most leadership books will tell you to do more.
Push harder.
Wake up earlier.
Optimize your way to fulfillment.

This book isn't about doing more.
It's about doing *different*.

Because what you're craving isn't another tool, title, or tactic.

What you're craving is clarity—the radical kind.

The kind that lets you finally say:
"This is who I am. This is what I see. This is what I'm building, and I'm not asking for permission."

If you feel like you've outgrown the version of success you spent years earning . . .
If you've been secretly asking, "What happened to my fire?"
If your outer life looks like a highlight reel but your inner world feels like a checklist . . .

You're not alone.
And you're not crazy for wanting more.

You're ready to lead a different way.

- In these pages, we'll move through the Strategic Unruliness™ framework:

- Get Radically Clear—*name what actually matters*, even when it's uncomfortable.
- Find Your Limits—spot the invisible rules you didn't know you were still following.
- Challenge the Rules—break what no longer serves, with precision.
- Expand Capacity—lead from the full force of who you are.

You'll find stories, reframes, fire starters, and body-based practices. Tools to help you shift, act, and lead differently. Starting now.

Because this isn't about motivation.
It's about liberation.

And liberation isn't a solo act.
Every time one person leads from truth instead of performance—
It chips away at the system that told us to shrink.

This is how change spreads:
One leader. One choice. One rule broken at a time.

Here's what that liberation actually looks like:

From	To
Performing success	**EMBODYING PURPOSE**
Hustling to prove	**LEADING WITH PRECISION**
Managing perception	**MOVING FROM RADICAL CLARITY**
Tolerating misalignment	**CREATING REAL RESONANCE**
Contorting to fit	**EXPANDING YOUR FULL RANGE**
Leading from fear	**LEADING WITH VISION**
Carrying it all	**LETTING GO OF WHAT DOESN'T BELONG**

And if something hits a nerve or opens a door and you don't know what to do next?

REACH OUT. SERIOUSLY. YOU'RE NOT DOING THIS ALONE.

If this resonates, if your chest tightens reading this, if you've been quietly asking, "Is this it?"
If you're tired of leading from the part of you that looks good on paper but feels hollow in real life—

Then you already know:

You're meant to build something bigger, braver, and more honest. Something that reflects who you really are, not only what you've been praised for.

And this?

THIS IS WHERE IT BEGINS.

Welcome to Strategic Unruliness™. Let's go.

PART I:
The Unraveling

CHAPTER ONE:

Exposed

It's 2007. I'm standing in the unairconditioned, stale-smelling bathroom at the Missouri Supreme Court, gripping the cold white porcelain sink like it's the only thing keeping me upright. My blouse is soaked through with sweat, not just from the heat. I'm trying not to puke.

Moments earlier, I delivered the highest stakes argument of my legal career. Now, under cruel fluorescent lights, I'm face-to-face with a pale, cracked version of myself. And all I can think is: It's over.

On paper, I'm unstoppable. Youngest partner in the firm. Record-breaking settlements. I walk into courtrooms and win. The woman they bring in when everything's on the line. Crisp. Controlled. Calculated. A winning machine in heels.

But machines don't feel. And I was feeling everything.

What no one saw: I was living a split life.

And here's the truth I hadn't told anyone:

No matter what I achieved, it was never enough. Not to fill the ache. The ache of being applauded for a version of me I knew wasn't the whole truth.

I was winning yet still wondering why I felt so hollow. I had everything I was supposed to want: the title, the cases, the respect. But behind the achievements was a quiet, relentless question:

Is this it?

That question didn't scream. It whispered. But it never stopped.
And because I couldn't name it, I started to believe I was the problem. That I was broken. Ungrateful. Fucked up for wanting something more.

So, I found an outlet. A hidden one.

Three times a month, I told colleagues I was visiting family. I packed rhinestones in my carry-on and flew around the country to compete in Latin ballroom dance competitions.

Not to escape power—to reclaim it.

In court, I was sharp, precise, and controlled. On the dance floor, I was heat. Rhythm. Command without apology.

I didn't just move. I owned every inch of space I entered. Hair down. Back arched. Eyes locked. The kind of presence that didn't ask for approval. It demanded attention.

This wasn't soft. It was feminine power at full voltage. Wild. Magnetic. Unedited.

I trained. I performed. I reigned. But only in secret.

Because in the world I came from—law firms, courtrooms, high-stakes strategy sessions—there was no room for radiance. You could be brilliant. You could be ruthless. But vulnerability? Wholeness? Soul? That shit didn't belong.

No one asked if their litigator could also rumba. No one cared who I was when the heels came off; only who I could be in a suit.

So, I split myself. The lawyer and the dancer. The strategist and the siren. The version they respected . . . and the one that made me feel alive.

And I told no one. Because it wasn't only *dance*. It was joy. It was truth. And the truth felt dangerous. But hiding it didn't protect me. It eroded me.

So, when my well-meaning husband leaned in and said with pride, "Your honors, I am so proud to introduce you to my wife and law partner, Kim. Not only is she an incredible attorney, but she's also a nationally ranked Latin dancer."—I froze.

Not metaphorically. Literally.

The Justices smiled. One raised an eyebrow. Another leaned back like he was settling in for a show. No words. Glances, sharp as glass.

My body? Numb. Feet moving on instinct. Voice on autopilot. Mind detached.

Dissociation isn't poetic. It's terrifying. I could hear myself speaking, feel my mouth forming words. But it was like I was floating outside my body, watching someone else perform. I was unraveling in real time.

And when it's over, I bolt. Straight to this bathroom. Gripping this sink. Holding myself up.

Because at this moment, I don't feel powerful. I feel exposed.

What I fear: They'll see the dancer and forget the lawyer. They'll see sparkle and think soft. They'll see color and discredit my clarity.

I don't hear the door open. But I feel her presence.

A Justice.

"Oh, good, you're here!" she beams.

Beams.

"I heard what your husband said, that you're a dancer. I think that is fabulous. I've always wanted to learn. Tell me everything. Where do you train? What kind of dance? I'm so impressed."

She says it like it's the most delightful thing she's heard all day.

I blink.

Here I was, unraveling, certain my secret had cost me everything. And she saw me as more. More human. More whole. More real.

That moment didn't fix everything. But it cracked something open.

A hairline fracture in the glass. Barely visible but irreversible. And once something cracks, the truth can finally begin to seep through.

At the time, I didn't think, "Maybe this is power." Honestly, I thought, "Maybe I don't have to hide." That was enough.

The rest came later—the clarity, the reclaiming, the shift.

But that moment? That was the beginning.

Maybe . . . you have your version of this, too.

Maybe yours isn't dance. Maybe it's painting. Writing. Hiking alone in the woods. Hosting wild, soulful dinners. Laughing too loudly. Dreaming too boldly. Loving too deeply.

Maybe there's something you love that no one at work even knows about because it doesn't fit their image of who you're supposed to be.

But that part of you? The one you save for weekends or whisper about only to your closest friend.

That might be the most powerful part of you.

The one that doesn't perform but commands. Doesn't please but leads.

That's where Strategic Unruliness™ was born.

Not in a boardroom. Not on a mountaintop. But in a courthouse bathroom. From the quiet realization that I was done splitting myself in half to belong.

No more shrinking. No more performance. No more hiding the parts of me that didn't match the mold.

If I were going to lead, it would now encompass all of me. Glitter and grit.

And that's where this begins. Not in strategy. But in the mirror. In the moment you choose to be whole.

You might read this and know instantly where you're holding back and hiding, and feel ready to jump into Strategic Unruliness™. Or, if you're like me, this has been a long time coming.

And I want you to know: *No single moment can change your life on a dime.* To arrive at the place where I am now—gratefully sitting and writing this book to make your journey infinitely easier than mine—I survived humiliation, heartbreak, and even failure. I held my ground when I wanted to crumble.

Moments so embarrassing, I nearly quit before I began. One of those moments still lives in my bones.

(circa 1995) I walked into the courtroom and didn't even know which podium was mine. Wall to wall with seasoned attorneys. And me? First motion argument. Ever.

I'll wait and see what the others do, I thought. I'll be fine.

First case called: Me.

I waited for opposing counsel to take his spot. Then I claimed mine.

"May it please the court . . ." I began.

The entire courtroom erupted in laughter. Apparently, that's not how we start motion arguments in California. I didn't know.

The judge's eyes narrowed. He was known for being particularly cruel. Now he knew he had a newbie.

Still, I continued. Tentatively. "I'm here to argue on behalf of my client under Statute section . . ." Whatever the hell I said.

"Young lady," he interrupted, drawing out every syllable like a warning.

"That statute does not apply."

Silence.

I had been handed the file ten minutes before leaving for court. I didn't know if it applied. I only knew I was in trouble.

He kept going. Louder this time.

"You come into my courtroom, unprepared, citing irrelevant statutes . . . wasting MY time?"

I was so pissed at myself. So embarrassed. So exposed.

I was seconds away from becoming a puddle on the floor. I felt like the whole room was waiting for me to break.

I knew Judge Haber was.

And perhaps it was that knowledge that saved me.

Because I didn't break, and I didn't crumble. I stood tall. Still. Unyielding.

Using my body to project a power I absolutely did not feel.

After what felt like minutes (probably seconds) of silence, I asked, calmly, for time to prepare and resubmit my motion.

His eyes narrowed one more time, and he begrudgingly said yes, warning me to NEVER again show up in his courtroom unprepared.

And just like that, it was over.

I fled the courtroom and let the tears come as soon as I reached the parking lot. I wanted to disappear. To never return to court.

I wasn't made for this.

Except, I was.

I cried hard. For a good long time. Eventually, I dried my tears and realized I was still standing. And rewrote the damn motion.

What comes after that moment? The moment when you fail miserably, publicly, spectacularly?

I'm going to be honest with you. It's horrible. It's every bit as bad as you imagine. Sometimes, it's worse.

Fuck the people who tell you failing "isn't so bad." Yes. It. Is.

But here's what you must know, the unfiltered truth: *Failing is the best thing that can happen to you.*

Because when you fail, you realize you can survive it. You understand that no matter what happens, you can choose to stand back up.

No amount of affirmation or positive self-talk will prove what you're made of like falling on your ass.

And if you're building something that's never been done before—even if you're deep in your genius, using every ounce of your gifts—chances are, you're going to hit some rough patches.

You have to know you've got what it takes. I know you do. *But you have to know it too.*

And the best way to be sure? Give yourself the privilege of not always getting it right. To be okay with failing and to see it for the gift it is.

That day in court? One of the worst days of my professional life. Also, one of the best.

Because it proved something no win ever did: *I could survive the worst-case scenario.*

And sometimes, that's all you need to start: A single moment that shows you what you're made of.

You don't need to be flawless to lead. You simply need to be whole.

Strategic Unruliness™ isn't about being fearless. It's about being real in rooms that taught you to perform.

If you've ever felt like you had to hide what's most true to be taken seriously, you're not alone.

This is your invitation to stop performing. And start leading as all of you.

It's going to be messy, uncomfortable, and uncharted.

If you're happy with how things are, this is not the book for you. But if you're done living someone else's version of your life?

Buckle up.

THE ROADMAP AHEAD

Strategic Unruliness™ is the path forward. Not a mindset. Not a vibe. A framework, built to help you reclaim your voice, your power, and your leadership.

Not by adding more to your plate, but by stripping away everything that doesn't belong.

Here's how it works:

GET RADICALLY CLEAR—on what matters, even when it's uncomfortable.
FIND YOUR LIMITS—spot the invisible rules you didn't know you were still following.

CHALLENGE THE RULES—break what no longer serves, with precision.

EXPAND CAPACITY—lead from the full force of who you are.

Each chapter will walk you through a piece of this path and offer fire starters to act, not just reflect.

Because this isn't only about motivation. You've got that. It's about momentum.

Let's get unruly.

UNRULY CHALLENGE™
The Split

What's the version of you that leads and the version you tuck away?

1. What do you love that you hide?
2. What truth rarely makes it into the room?
3. What are you scared they'll misunderstand?

Write it. Say it. Let it breathe. Because every time you split yourself to fit, you leave power on the table.

UNRULY MOVE™
Wholeness Over Performance

Choose wholeness, even when it feels risky. Because every time you tell the truth about who you are, you break a rule that never served you in the first place.

Let's go.

Interlude
I'M TWO IN THE AIR

I was three. Traveling from Reno back to St. Louis with my great aunt and uncle. My parents were in the middle of a divorce. Money was tight.

Apparently, two-year-olds didn't need to pay for plane fare.

So, they coached me: "If anyone asks, you're two."

I was proud to be three years old. Really proud. That number meant something to me.

Somewhere above Kansas, a flight attendant leaned in close. "You're such a cute little girl. How old are you?"

I looked her straight in the eye. "I'm two in the air, and three on the ground."

That line says it all.

Even as a toddler, I knew when I was being asked to perform a version of myself that wasn't quite true. That my value might depend on saying the right thing. Hiding the whole truth. Being strategic about my answers.

That moment became a blueprint: Shape the story. Protect the people. Bend the truth if it makes things easier.

And if you must split yourself in two to fit the circumstances, do it with a smile.

I was trained early to shape-shift for acceptance.

But now? We're writing new rules, where your full self doesn't just belong, it leads.

CHAPTER TWO:

The Rules That Raised You

Most of the rules you follow? You never chose them. You inherited them. Absorbed them. Learned to perform them to survive. But what helped you belong might be the very thing keeping you small. And now? You're done shrinking.

I was two. My sister, only a few months old. And my mom—newly divorced, barely standing, and somehow still moving us forward. We had just left Reno, Nevada. For reasons I wouldn't understand until much later—and only through her lens of truth—we wouldn't be living with our dad anymore. She packed us up, carried the weight, and drove us halfway across the country to St. Louis. To start over. To stay with her parents. To survive.

Most of my early childhood is a blur—fractured memories, half-stories. But this night? This one is seared into me.

We stopped for the night at a roadside motel, the kind with rusty railings and a diner across the parking lot. We were tired. Hungry. Frayed. My mom didn't eat. I had a chocolate milkshake—a rare, golden-bright treat. My sister whimpered in her arms while we sat in that booth. Silence sat with us at that table, heavier than any plate of food. We weren't quiet because we wanted to be. We were quiet because everything hurt.

Back at the lobby, my mom stopped suddenly. Her breath caught. "My purse," she said, her voice cracking. She'd left it at the restaurant.

Her whole face collapsed.

Her wallet—the one thing that could get us to "home," whatever that meant now—was sitting on a sticky vinyl seat across a dark parking lot. My sister started crying. My mom looked around helplessly, panic tightening everything.

And then she looked at me.

"Kim, honey. You're my brave girl, aren't you?"

I nodded eagerly. "Yes, Mommy."

"I need you to do something for me, and I'll be right here, okay? I need you to go back to the restaurant and get my purse. It's where we were sitting. Can you do that for me?"

"Yes."

I was so proud. Of course I could. Of course I would. I was a helper. I was brave. I was two years old.

But as I started to walk across the parking lot, my feeling of pride turned to fear.

The restaurant felt farther than I remembered. The sky darker. The pavement bigger. I stopped for a moment, turning my little body ever so slightly and tentatively looking back over my right shoulder.

My mom, holding my sister tightly in her arms, nodded her encouragement. Soft smile. Wet eyes. Silent plea.

I took a shaky breath. Steadied myself. And kept going.

To this day, I'm not sure how I remember that walk in such vivid detail. It seems impossible that I do. And yet, I can pull it from my memory and play it like an old movie, frame by frame.

The glow of the parking lot lights. The hum of the neon sign. The uneven thud of my tiny shoes on cracked pavement.

I remember climbing into the booth, reaching for the oversized purse—heavy and brown and enormous in my arms—and carrying it back, as carefully as I could, like it held the fate of the world.

Because in some ways, it did. It held our hope. Our future. Our chance to make it through the next day.

That was the night I made a decision I couldn't have named at the time. A contract—invisible, but binding: It's my job to fix it. To make it okay. To be the one they can count on.

That moment taught me: My safety comes from being brave. Being capable. Being the solution.

And it doesn't matter if you were two years old or twenty. Some of us made the same deal: I'll stay strong if you stay safe. I'll disappear if it keeps the peace. I'll be perfect if it gets me love. That contract doesn't ask for your permission. But it does demand your energy.

That's how the rules get in.

And here's what no one tells you: Rules absorbed in moments like this don't stay in the moment. They follow you. Quietly. Relentlessly.

They shaped how I used to lead. Over-functioning and calling it "excellence." Showing up early, staying up late, and fixing everyone's problems before being asked. Being the one they relied on—the fixer, the anchor, the answer—even when it drained me completely.

And maybe you've done it too, become the glue, the fixer, the steady one, because you didn't think you had another choice. The rules shape what you tolerate . . . others asking you to sacrifice yourself for their benefit, in the name of loyalty or acceptance. They shape what you believe you deserve, believing you have to earn love, success, and even joy.

All because a younger version of you made a deal to survive, for love, or for acceptance. And once that deal is made, it doesn't ask for permission to keep running. It becomes background code—shaping your decisions, your desires, your limits—until you name it.

Maybe your moment didn't happen in a parking lot. Maybe it happened at a dinner table. On a stage. In a locker room. A boardroom. A hospital hallway. Maybe it wasn't one moment, but a slow accumulation . . . nods, looks, silences that taught you what was safe to be, and what had to stay hidden.

But you have a version of this. And it matters.

Because when you name the rules and how they got in, you can start by deciding which ones have to go.

Sometimes they're unspoken. Sometimes they're loud and clear. Either way, they land. And they stick.

And just because they came from people we love doesn't mean they were right. Just because they helped us survive doesn't mean they're meant to stay.

Most of the rules shaping your life? You never agreed to them. You didn't write them. You didn't vote. You didn't choose them. But you follow them anyway.

Rules about how to lead. How to speak. How to look. How to be. How to win. How to hide. How to perform strength while suppressing need.

Rules about how to sacrifice yourself to provide, and your need to take care of everyone else's wants.

Rules like:

> Be grateful, not ambitious.
> Be capable, not disruptive.
> Be logical, not emotional.
> Never admit you're lost.
> Protect others from your pain.
> Be accommodating, not demanding.
> Be polished, not powerful.
> Be the solution, not the problem.
> Make it look easy, no matter how hard it is.
> Be busy, not boundaried.
> Carry the weight without complaint.
> Grind to prove your worth because ease is laziness.
> Strength means silence.
> Don't need too much.
> Don't want too much.
> Don't take up too much space.
> Don't ask for more than you're given.
> Don't question what you've been told is enough.
> Don't believe too deeply that something bigger might be meant for you.
> Don't dream too big because you'll only be disappointed.

And so many more.

Some were spoken out loud. Others absorbed in silence. But every single one became part of how you learned to belong, be liked, and succeed.

Some were written in pencil. Invisible to most, easy to deny.
Others were carved into your skin.

Gender. Race. Age. Accent. Body. Neurodivergence. Background.

If you've had to work twice as hard to be taken half as seriously, that's not personal. That's structural.

And it's not yours to carry alone.

This is why clarity isn't only personal, it's cultural.
When you find the limit and say, *"That doesn't belong to me,"* you don't just reclaim your power. You model what's possible for everyone still stuck inside it.

And here's the quiet truth about rules like these: They don't make you safer. They make you smaller. They work . . . until they don't. Until the cost of staying small becomes greater than the risk of breaking free.

That's what we're doing here: *naming the rules to challenge them.*

Because that's your right. You get to decide what still serves you and what never did.

Because the moment you stop obeying someone else's rulebook, you start writing your own.

And when you write a new rule, you don't just change your life:

You create permission for someone else to do the same.

That's how a movement begins. One leader. One decision. One shift at a time.

Here's what else you need to know: Rules always work best for the people who make them. Rules are outdated by design. They reflect the status quo that's already been lived. Rules don't know your gifts, your brilliance, or your future. Rules weren't made for you. They were made to keep systems intact. Rules don't expand your potential; they contain it. Rules can only take you so far and never where you're meant to go.

So, if the rules don't feel right anymore, it's not because you're broken. It's because you're waking up.

UNRULY CHALLENGE™
Name the Rules

Name the rules that feel like laws, the ones you've never thought to question. The ones that shaped how you show up, what you say yes to, and what you believe is possible. Then ask yourself:

1. Where did this rule come from?
2. Whose comfort did I protect by following it?
3. What part of me did this rule keep small?

Because the moment you can name the rule, you can begin to challenge it. And that's where everything starts to shift.

UNRULY MOVE™
Say It Out Loud

Take one rule you've identified, and say it out loud. Not to break it yet, but to disarm it. Say: *"This is a rule I've been following, and I get to decide if it stays."* Owning your awareness is the first act of power. You don't need to fix it or flip it overnight. You need to name it out loud so it loses its grip. Because the rules that feel most absolute are often the ones we never chose.

Interlude
RECKLESS ROOTS

We lived on the edge of civilization. Rural county. Few people. Fewer rules.

By 13, I was put in charge of my little sister every Saturday night while our parents went out. I didn't love it. I wanted candy.

The mall was ten minutes away. And I decided: I could drive. No license. No practice. No permission. Just belief and motivation.

It was dark. The roads were winding. My sister cried the whole way there and back. I made her sit on the rear floorboard, so she'd be an accomplice.

I gripped the wheel, heart pounding, and drove us to the mall. For Junior Mints.

And you know what? I pulled it off. Didn't crash. Didn't get caught. Got my candy.

It was reckless. Irresponsible. And weirdly empowering.

That wasn't conviction. That was compulsion. Now I know the difference.

Conviction isn't only doing what no one expects. It's doing what must be done even when no one else sees it yet.

That's the shift. From impulse to impact. From rebellion to real leadership.

You already feel it. Now, we build it.

CHAPTER THREE:

The Hidden Cost of Obedience

You feel it in your chest. A tightening when you stay quiet.
Heat rising when you're dismissed. The hollow ache after
a meeting where you swallowed what you knew. It's not just
frustration. It's grief. Grief for every moment you made yourself
smaller to be taken seriously. For every truth you buried to protect
someone else's comfort. For how long you've been holding
it all and calling it strength. No more.

I was the newest lawyer on the team. The only woman. Sitting in a conference room filled with senior litigators—all male, all older—strategizing for trial.

The conversation was buzzing. They were prepping to cross-examine the opposing side's key witness, a woman who had shown emotion in her deposition. Anger, they said. She's going to turn the jury off. This is how we go after her.

They were unanimous. Fired up. A sea of "Exactly," and "Dead on," echoing around the room.

Here's what they didn't know: *They were wrong.*

I had watched the same deposition, and what I saw wasn't anger. It was grief. This woman wasn't defensive; she was devastated. And if they attacked her on the stand, it would make the jury empathize with her.

I felt it in my body. The temperature rising in my cheeks. The knowing tightening in my gut.

I opened my mouth to speak. To challenge the plan. To offer an alternative.

And then I shut it.

Because I had learned the rules: You're here, but not to contribute. To observe. Fetch menus. Smile and take notes. You don't interrupt. You don't correct. You haven't earned that yet, and probably never will.

Swallowing my words stung, sharp and bitter, like biting my own tongue.

But I stayed quiet.

The next day in court, it played out exactly as I knew it would. They went after her. She broke down, and the jury leaned in, not away.

We lost the case.

For years, I questioned my decision not to speak up. Should I have said something? Would it have mattered?

In the end, I let myself off the hook. No chance they would have listened to me.

But if the rules enforcing the law firm hierarchy hadn't been so firmly ingrained, and my input had been welcome, a client might not have lost $20 million.

That's what the rules cost, among other things.

How many times have you failed to speak when you knew the answer? How many times have you swallowed your insight because you hadn't "earned it yet?" How much has that silence actually cost?

THE SOUL COST—SPLITTING TO SURVIVE

The part of you that once spoke freely—the truth-teller, the knower, the spark—gets muted. Not because it's gone, but because it's been rewired for safety. That's the soul cost: losing connection to your own clarity in the name of staying acceptable. When you shrink to fit a rule, you lose contact with your own knowing. The part that sees clearly. The instinct that would've spoken up. The insight that could've changed everything.

Whether in heels or a suit, a boardroom or a Zoom square, every time you contort to be acceptable, professional, promotable, you teach your nervous system that safety costs authenticity. You wire yourself for silence.

And that silence? It becomes a habit. A posture. A personality.

But it was never you.

It was a strategy for survival.

And it works . . . until it doesn't.

Until the gap between who you are and how you show up becomes a chasm. Until the weariness isn't from work—it's from pretending.

THE INNOVATION COST—KILLING THE EDGE

Rules sterilize culture. Period. You can feel it in the room: safe but stagnant, filled with nodding heads and dead eyes. The kind of space where ideas go to be approved, not born.

Innovation doesn't die in failure. It dies in meetings where no one says what they're really thinking. It dies in leaders who know the truth and stay quiet. It dies in companies where compliance is rewarded more than courage.

The cost? Edge. Vision. The thing that could've made you unmissable.

You don't change the game by playing it better. You change it by asking why we're playing it this way at all.

THE GENERATIONAL COST—TEACHING SILENCE

The rules you follow aren't neutral. They teach.

They teach your team how much truth is allowed. They teach your mentees how much is too much. They teach your kids what leadership looks like and what it hides.

Every time you override your gut to keep the peace, someone else learns that their gut isn't trustworthy.

Every time you swallow a truth to protect someone's comfort, you reinforce the idea that discomfort is dangerous.

Every time you perform instead of lead, you give others a script, not permission.

And that script becomes law.

Unless you break it.

THE SYSTEMIC COST—UPHOLDING WHAT HURTS YOU

Most of the rules weren't made for your liberation. They were made for your compliance.

And when you follow them without question, you uphold the very systems that never accounted for your full self.

This is the most brutal truth to name: Sometimes the rules that feel safest are the ones causing the most damage.

Because they keep you in rooms that weren't built for you, chasing standards that weren't designed for you, and performing identities that drain you.

They tell you: Play it safe, and you'll rise.

But they never say what you'll lose on the way up.

THE UNTAPPED POTENTIAL—THE LIFE THAT NEVER GETS LIVED

This is the real cost.

The book you don't write. The business you don't build. The vision you never say out loud.

Because you were waiting. For approval. For timing. For proof.

But you don't need more evidence; you simply need your own permission.

Because if you stay inside rules that were never made for your greatness, you will spend your whole life performing someone else's version of success.

Strategic Unruliness™ isn't rebellion for rebellion's sake. It's how you reclaim the life that's actually yours.

So, ask yourself: *Are you still biting your tongue, nodding along, or playing it safe?* And, if so, what would it take to stop?

And it starts here: What is the rule that's costing you the most? And are you willing to challenge it before it costs you everything?

UNRULY CHALLENGE™
Make the Cost Visible

Write down one rule you've been following. Then name its actual cost. Not just the stress. The loss.

1. What has it stolen?
2. What has it silenced?
3. What has it delayed?

UNRULY MOVE™
Break One Rule on Purpose

Not recklessly. Not dramatically. Just intentionally. Pick one rule that no longer serves. *Break it in service of something more true.* And notice what rushes in when you do. This is where your brilliance begins.

Interlude
AM I INVISIBLE?

Invisibility doesn't only happen to women, but let's be real, it happens to us a lot.

I spoke up with an idea. A good one. Sharp. Strategic. The kind that solves the problem and opens a path.

Silence.

Then, moments later, a man across the table repeated it.
Almost word for word.

"Brilliant," someone said. "Exactly what we need," echoed another.

And I sat there thinking: *What the fuck? Am I invisible?*

That moment didn't just sting. It made me question everything.

Because if your ideas only count when someone else delivers them, it's not about merit. It's about power.

And I've seen it in men too- the quiet ones who lead with vision but never raise their voice, who get sidelined for not playing the bravado game. Who wonders if power must always mean performance?

And the rules? They're rigged to decide who gets heard.

CHAPTER FOUR:

Unraveling in Real Time

You've played the part for so long, they think it's who you are. Capable. Controlled. Strategic. Safe. But here's the truth no one sees: You are not just this role. You are fire. Depth. Instinct. Power. Wholeness. And you're done editing yourself to be understood by people who only know the surface. You're done performing.
It's time to break the script.

Last Tuesday, Kate stood in front of her closet for twenty-six minutes. Not because she didn't have clothes. But because nothing felt like her. Not the designer blazer that screamed credibility. Not the heels that added power with every step. Not even the go-to navy sheath that had sealed million-dollar deals and earned silent nods of respect in every boardroom.

Everything felt like a costume. She called me and said, "This sucks. I should be excited, and I want to go back to bed. I want to be anywhere but here."

Sound familiar? Maybe for you, it's not a pitch. It's a team meeting, a parent conference, a boardroom, a birthday. But that same ache? It's there. You're not alone.

Kate is a powerhouse. She had a high-stakes pitch that morning, one she was known for. Clients flew in for her. Teams lit up when she spoke. Her name opened doors. She was at the top of her game.

And yet, as she got dressed, her chest tightened. Her hands trembled. Her skin felt like it didn't quite fit.

Not from fear. From something trickier to name. A creeping hollowness. A sense that she was slipping further and further away from herself.

She still nailed the pitch. Her team raved. The client signed. Everyone called her unstoppable.

But in the car afterward, with the radio off and her hands still clenched at ten and two, she stared blankly through the windshield and thought: *Why do I feel nothing?*

She used to come alive in rooms like that. Now she was watching her life like a silent reel. Nothing was wrong. And somehow, everything was.

It doesn't always hit like a breakdown. Sometimes it's quieter. Slower. Like a subtle hum in the background of your life that gets harder to ignore.

A heaviness in your chest when you open your laptop. A sudden blank stare when someone asks how you're doing. A constant, low-grade ache that whispers, *"This isn't working"*. Even when everything looks like it is.

It's not burnout. Not exactly. It's more like a slow erosion of alignment.

And if you've felt it, you know.

This emptiness doesn't care what's on your business card or in your bank account. I've seen it hit founders, creatives, operators—anyone who's mastered the mechanics but lost the meaning.

You know what it's like to wake up in a life you built and wonder how much of yourself you had to bury to build it. You've followed the rules. Checked the boxes. Done everything they told you would lead to a good life.

And yet, you can't shake the sense that something vital has gone missing. That maybe, somehow, in becoming who everyone needed you to be, the real you started vanishing.

I call it the feeling of "un-something." Not a diagnosis. Not a crisis. A quiet, persistent signal that something in you is evolving, and your life hasn't caught up yet.

But we're not taught to listen to that feeling. We're taught to silence it. To override it. To label it as weak, ungrateful, and dramatic. We're told to push through. To stay grateful. To focus on how lucky we are.

And so, we learn to doubt it. To mistrust the very voice inside us that's trying to lead us forward.

But what if that ache isn't a problem to fix? What if it's clarity in disguise, your deeper truth, knocking for your attention?

The feeling of "un-something" doesn't mean you're falling apart. It means something deeper in you is waking up. It means you're starting to outgrow the version of success you were handed.

If you let yourself pay attention, even just a little, that ache becomes a signal. Not to burn everything down. But to stop pretending. To be honest. To notice what no longer fits.

This is your moment. Not to push harder. But to finally tell the truth about what's no longer working, and start listening to the feeling that's been trying to guide you.

You don't need to solve it yet. You just need to hear it. Listen to it. Don't look away. Whatever it's telling you, it's not wrong. It's your truth trying to break through. Let it lead you to your limits. Because that's where the shift begins.

For some, it feels like being unfulfilled. For others, unmotivated. Uninspired. Unaligned. Unseen. There's no single definition, only the truth that something inside you is evolving. It's your soul's version of an overdue software update.

Mine showed up in the form of guilt. Shame, even. I felt guilty for dancing, for having something that was mine. It had a lot to do with why I didn't let anyone know I did it at all. I didn't deserve something just for me. I had to earn everything. It all had to be hard.

I remember writing a letter to my adopted grandparents telling them how grateful I was that their son had adopted me. I hoped it would make them love me. That it would shift something. That they'd stop seeing us as burdens and start seeing us as family.

It didn't work.

Because when I was little, I learned early and often that I shouldn't want too much. That more wasn't meant for me. That I should be grateful for what I had, and anything beyond that? Off-limits.

I was told I was lucky. Lucky to be adopted. Lucky someone took care of us. Lucky for every opportunity I had. And if I ever voiced a desire for more? I was met with one word: *ungrateful*.

So, naturally, wanting more always felt like a betrayal. A slap in the face of everything I'd been given. Even when that "more" wasn't selfish, just soul-driven.

We all have messages like that. Quiet scripts that tell us what we're allowed to want. Who we are supposed to be. And they don't usually come from cruelty. Most of the time, they're someone else's pain. Someone else's fear, projected onto us. Handed down like heirlooms.

But just because it wasn't meant to hurt us, doesn't mean it didn't land. Pain doesn't have to be intentional to be powerful.

And here we are—grown, accomplished, outwardly thriving—still feeling like shit for wanting more.

At first, I tried to outrun it. Achieve my way through it. I stacked up wins like armor. Took on the toughest cases. Crushed the billable hours. Earned the bonuses. Built a reputation as the one who would always deliver under pressure. Played the role of the unshakable attorney who always came through.

But no number of big cases, courtroom wins, or legal accolades could quiet that whisper, and I'm not alone.

I've worked with leaders who carry entire companies on their shoulders, and still lie awake at night wondering why it all feels so hollow.

Research on high achievers has coined a term for this: achievement fatigue. A 2023 McKinsey study found that nearly 60% of high-performing leaders report feeling unfulfilled. Not unsuccessful—unfulfilled. That's not burnout. It's a soul signal: You've mastered a role that no longer fits. It's not failure; it's the gap between who you've had to be and *who you actually are.* There must be more than this.

And it wasn't until I started telling the truth about that whisper that things began to shift. Not overnight. But enough to breathe again. Enough to see that I wasn't broken. I was just out of alignment.

And here's the part I need you to hear: You are not ungrateful. You are not unstable. You are not asking for too much. You are waking up.

The feeling of un-something is not the problem. It's the invitation.

It means your inner world is evolving faster than the life you've built around it. And it's more common than you think, even among the highest performers. The feeling doesn't mean you're broken. It means you're outgrowing the old version of yourself.

And if you let it speak, if you stop trying to manage or dismiss or outperform it, that whisper becomes a compass.

It will take you to where no playbook can.

Because this isn't about fixing yourself, it's about finally seeing yourself. Unfiltered. Unedited. Undeniably whole.

UNRULY CHALLENGE™
Name Your "Un-Something"

Don't rush it. Don't fix it. Just name it. Is it unfulfilled? Unseen? Uninspired? Unaligned? Write it down. Sit with it. Let it speak. Then ask yourself:

1. Where am I performing instead of leading?
2. What part of me have I been editing out?
3. What would happen if I brought that version of me into the room?

This is your first act of Strategic Unruliness™: Not doing more, just telling the truth. And truth has a way of clearing the path. *When you start telling the truth, you begin to reclaim your clarity, your compass, your voice. Even when the truth is hard.*

Quick Example: One of my clients, let's call her Rachel, had built a wildly successful consultancy. She was exhausted and disengaged and couldn't figure out why. When she finally named her "un-something" as uninspired, it unlocked a massive shift. She didn't need to quit. She just needed to stop editing herself out of it. Within months, her work—and her team—came back to life. Naming the feeling was the catalyst. It gave her permission to stop performing and start rebuilding from *Truth*.

UNRULY MOVE™
Tell the Truth Before You Have the Plan

Tell the truth about what no longer fulfills you before you make the plan. Because clarity isn't the reward. It's the starting point. Ask yourself: Can I name one truth I've been avoiding, even from myself?

Sometimes the feeling of "un-something" isn't vague at all. Sometimes it's sharp, sudden, and lands like a gut punch.

Interlude
YOU KILLED JESUS
What Happens When Identity Becomes a Target

I was thirteen. Seventh grade. A sleepover with girls I thought were my friends.

We were giggling, snacking, telling stories. Then the conversation shifted. Someone asked what religion I was. I said, Jewish.

And just like that, the room turned.

"You killed Jesus," one of them said.

I thought she was joking. She wasn't.

They nodded. Another asked why I did it. One pulled out a Sunday school book—vivid illustrations of Jesus on the cross—and held it up like evidence.

I didn't come from a religious family. Spiritual, yes. But I'd never been told I had blood on my hands.

I was confused. Then, I was horrified. Then crying.

No one stood up for me. No one told her to stop. They just watched.

There were no cell phones back then. I asked to use the house phone, still sobbing. Her mom handed it to me. I called mine and said, "Please, you have to come get me. They said I killed Jesus."

Later, one or two whispered apologies. "I wanted to say something." "I didn't know what to do."

But by then, the fracture was permanent.

That night, I learned how fast belonging can vanish. How a single label can override a hundred shared experiences. How silence from the sidelines can feel worse than the insult itself.

I also learned this: We have so much more in common than what divides us. But only if we're brave enough to act like it.

Break the silence. Stand for what's right while it still matters.

We're not here to fit quietly. We're here to lead clearly, even when it's uncomfortable.

PART II:
The Reckoning

CHAPTER FIVE:

Say the Thing

*There's something in you that wants out. A truth. A vision.
A knowing. And the longer you hold it in, the louder it gets.
You don't need a plan yet. You just need to say it.
To see it and refuse to look away.*

Allison was frustrated. Not in a throw-a-chair kind of way, but in that quiet, simmering, stuck-in-the-weeds, everything-is-off-and-I-can't-quite-place-it kind of way.

Smart. Strategic. Experienced. She could see what needed to happen, but no one else seemed to be getting it. And that made her question everything.

She wasn't a tyrant, although sometimes people said she was, which felt really unfair to her. Because she wanted the best for everyone. She was just really tired. And most of all, she was discouraged.

She was in the weeds. Following up on missed deadlines. Triple-checking every client deliverable. Writing the emails herself because she didn't trust they'd get it right. Fixing mistakes that shouldn't have been made. Wondering how the hell this is still happening?

She'd built the business—a boutique event production company—high-touch, high-stakes, high-pressure. One mistake could tank the reputation she'd spent years building. And lately, it felt like balls were dropping left and right.

Some days, she was sure it was her team. Other days, she doubted herself. Maybe she wasn't clear. Maybe she wasn't as good a leader as she thought. Maybe she was expecting too much.

At night, she'd lie in bed replaying conversations. Decoding what she had said . . . or hadn't said. Wondering if she was too vague, too intense, too unrealistic.

She kept showing up. Kept pushing. Kept trying to lead with grace. But underneath, she was unraveling. She didn't feel like a visionary. She felt like a micromanager: clenched jaw, tight chest, haunted by the fear that maybe she was the bottleneck, not the brilliance. And that terrified her.

She told me they didn't care. That they weren't trying. That they were just collecting paychecks. That she was doing everything—carrying the weight, solving the problems, keeping the ship afloat—and they were coasting.

In fact? Her team was trying like hell to please her. They just couldn't win because her vision wasn't just unclear, it was unspoken. And it kept changing.

It was like aiming for a moving target in the dark.

That's what happens when clarity goes missing. You start mislabeling the problem. You blame the disengagement on laziness when it's really confusion. You take it personally. You wonder if it's even buildable. If it's them or you.

Misdiagnosed friction doesn't just drain results. It erodes confidence, the kind that shows up in darting eyes during meetings, in hesitations before offering ideas, in the growing silence where bold thinking used to live. Slowly. Quietly. Completely.

Allison believed she was being clear. But clarity isn't about effort or volume. And in this case, her clarity didn't land because it didn't exist.

Her team didn't understand the objectives. And they didn't know why they mattered or how their role fit the bigger picture.

And the truth? Neither did she. Not out loud. Not in a way that made the vision feel shared.

That's the part no one tells you about leadership: You can't assume they see what you see. You have to say it. Expectations shifted, but she didn't say so. Priorities changed, but she didn't explain why. The vision was clear in her head, but fuzzy in the room.

So, her team stopped guessing. And started playing it safe.

They weren't lazy. They were unclear. They didn't lack motivation. They lacked direction.

Before she could align the team, she had to be radically honest: *What did she really want?*

She thought she wanted more time. More balance. Less pressure.

So, she picked an old goal: to land five new corporate clients in Q1. Her team delivered six. Success on paper. Revenue spiked.

But when the numbers came in? *She felt numb.*

Everyone else celebrated. Her team beamed. They pitched their hearts out, and she smiled back. But the smile didn't reach her eyes. Her thank you felt flat. And everyone felt it.

Whispers started: "Did we miss something?" "Was that not what she wanted?"

That was Allison's wakeup moment. The heartbreak of success that did not feel like success.

The team hit the goal. But they didn't know the whole picture. And neither did she.

Because she didn't want volume, she wanted artistry. Transformation. Events that felt like magic, not polished logistics. And that shift—from performance goals to purpose-driven clarity—hadn't been spoken. Not even to herself.

She masked it with strategy talk: better systems, stronger processes. But the truth? She didn't think she could have what she really wanted.

Too big. Too bold. Too much.

Until she said it.

And when she did—not the goal she thought she should want, but the one she couldn't shake—everything shifted.

Her dream wasn't just hers. Her clients were craving the same thing. Connection. Story. Meaning. And her team? They were hungry to create something that mattered.

That's why radical clarity isn't a communication tactic. It's the foundation of Strategic Unruliness™.

We made one shift: *She started saying what she saw.*

Not just what she wanted. But, instead, why it mattered. What great looked like. How every team member played a part.

She said: "Here's the long game I'm playing; not just Q1, but legacy." "Here's what this phase requires and why it matters more than ever." "Here's what excellence looks like and why I know we can rise to meet it."

She stopped assuming clarity and started confirming it: "What did you hear as the goal?" "What matters most in this to you?" "What could get in the way, and how can I help?"

That shift? *It changed everything.*

Clarity didn't just improve communication. It made the work meaningful. Engagement soared. Trust deepened. Momentum returned.

Because people don't resist leadership, they resist confusion.

And then there was Jason.

Ex-military, now COO of a global logistics firm. Sharp, precise, and exhausted.

He called me one night and said, "I'm tired of being the guy who always knows what to do. I don't even know what I want anymore."

The truth wasn't in the tactics. It was in the silence.
And once he named it? Everything shifted.

You can't lead toward something you're afraid to name.
If it's your vision, your dream, your idea—say the damn thing.

Don't shrink your dream to fit what's possible.
Don't water it down to make it palatable.
You don't need permission to want what you want.

A lighthouse doesn't go chasing ships. It shines.

And great leaders, like lighthouses, don't chase; they clarify.
They light the way so that the right people can find them.

That's your job.

Shine. Get clear. Let the right people find you.

Because when your people know the why and see themselves inside of it, they stop performing. They start owning.

That's clarity.
That's leadership.
That's the first unruly act.

The Two Whys You Need

Your vision needs two whys:
THE PERSONAL WHY—This is about you. What lights you up, drives you, moves you. It's what gives your vision its soul.
THE CUSTOMER WHY—This is about them. The people you serve. Why it matters to them. Why it solves their problem, meets their desire, or changes their experience. This is what gives your vision traction.

Most leaders confuse these or collapse them into one. But clarity means naming both.

Because if your vision only lights you up, it risks becoming self-serving. And if it only serves others but doesn't light you up, it becomes hollow.

You need both. Truth and traction. Soul and strategy. That's how vision becomes a movement.

Because without a steady pulse of vision, direction, and truth, any rebellious move is just static in the signal. If you don't tell the truth about what matters, breaking the rules won't free you. It'll just create more chaos.

Strategic Unruliness™ starts with radical clarity, not as a nice-to-have, but as a prerequisite. Because saying the real thing—before it's perfect, before it's popular—always challenges someone's rule.

UNRULY CHALLENGE™
Face What's Risky

What's the thing you haven't fully named because it feels too big, too risky, or too much? Write it down. Say it out loud. Let it be true, even if you're not ready to act on it yet. Then ask yourself:

1. What have I been communicating instead?
2. What's the cost of staying vague?
3. What would become possible if I were crystal clear?

Because the clarity you're avoiding might be the clarity your team is craving.

UNRULY MOVE™
Say the Real Thing

Stop softening your vision to make it easier for people to accept. Say the real thing. Before it's perfect. Before it's proven. Before you earn permission. You don't need permission to lead from your truth. You need clarity—and the guts to speak it.

Interlude
SALSA DATE NIGHT

Every time I teach Salsa Date Night—a fun, low-stakes dance event for couples—I see the same thing happen.

They show up smiling. Ready for fun. And five minutes in, they're frustrated. Not because the steps are hard. But because one person is leading, and the other is trying to follow a lead that's unclear.

He steps forward. She hesitates. She spins. He wasn't ready. Timing's off. Feet get tangled. One partner pulls, and the other pushes. The laughter fades. The blame begins.

Even when they've agreed on who's leading and who's following, there's resistance. Why? Because clarity is hard. Especially in motion. Especially when emotions are involved.

If the lead doesn't move with intention and consistency, the follower can't follow. And if the follower makes a move the lead didn't expect, the lead feels inadequate or blames the follower for misreading them.

I've had to settle more couple-disputes over a simple forward-and-back salsa step than I ever expected.

Now imagine how this shows up at work. In meetings. In strategy shifts. In moments of pressure.

Clarity isn't just about communication. It's about rhythm, timing, and trust. Without it, even simple steps become collisions.

And if this sounds familiar, it's because the same tension shows up in every leadership team. When leaders aren't clear on their role, rhythm, or why, people stop dancing. They freeze, they push, they pull. Clarity is the beat that makes the whole thing move.

In dance, and leadership, the problem usually isn't the follower. *It's the lead.*

So, if your team isn't moving with you, don't blame the dance. Check your lead. Say what you see.

CHAPTER SIX:

Say the Fucking Thing
(Even on LinkedIn)

I knew it might cost me something that mattered.
Not my job. Not my livelihood.
But something sneakier and harder to name.
The reach. The traction.
The quiet algorithmic nod that says, "You're doing it right."

All I had to do to keep it?
Play nice.
Soften the edges.
Swap "fuckup" for "fail."
Make it cleaner. Easier to digest. Easier to ignore.

That's what they told me:
"LinkedIn doesn't like that word."
"You're gonna get buried."
"Just call it Friday Fail. You'll be fine."

But I wasn't here to be fine.
I was here to be real. Aligned. Strategic—and unruly.

So, I posted it anyway.
The first Friday Fuckup.

No euphemisms. No spin. Just a raw, honest reflection on a moment that didn't go the way I hoped and what I learned from it.

And LinkedIn?
Silent.
Low views. Dead reach.
A polite slap on the wrist from the invisible content police.

I'd broken the rule.

And then came the whisper: "Maybe you should pull back."
"Maybe it's too much."
"Maybe next time, play it safer."

But the question in my gut was louder: *Do I shrink to fit the feed?*
Or speak to the people who matter?

The following Friday, I posted again.
Same title. Same voice. Same unapologetic truth.

And this time?
It blew up.
Over 40,000 views in two days.
Hundreds of comments.
A flood of DMs saying, "Thank you."
"I thought I was the only one."
"You just gave me permission to be honest."

And then I posted about egg whites in my coffee. A tiny moment of real life. The kind of moment most people would hide, but I shared it. Because it was real. Because it mattered. Because it was mine.

Over 80,000 views. More than 400 comments. People didn't just laugh, they connected. They opened up. They felt seen.

That's the point. Also, the proof: *It wasn't rebellion. It was resonance.*

This is Strategic Unruliness™ in action. Not rebellion for rebellion's sake. But leadership done real.

Because here's the thing:
Platforms are built on patterns. But movements are built on truth.

Most people are still filtering themselves into invisibility.
Polishing their voice until it's flavorless.
Conforming just enough to avoid friction, and in the process, erasing the one thing that could actually create connection.

But the moment I stopped writing for approval and started writing for impact, something shifted: *The right people showed up.*

Not because I followed the script.
But because I finally stopped believing that I needed one.

And that's the real unlock:
The right people don't come for your polish. They come for your power.

Strategic Unruliness™ doesn't mean saying everything all the time.
It means saying the real thing—on purpose.
Not to provoke.
But to reveal.
To realign.
To wake people up.

So, if you're feeling that tension between what you want to say and what you're "supposed" to, pause and ask:
What am I afraid it will cost me?
And what might it unlock instead?

Because every time you mute your voice to stay visible, you teach your audience to expect less truth.
Less clarity.
Less you.

And you weren't built to be less.

Say the fucking thing.
Not for the algorithm.
For the people.
For the future you're here to lead.

UNRULY CHALLENGE™
Say the Thing Anyway

1. What's the title, truth, or tension you've been softening?
2. What would happen if you said it exactly as it needs to be said?

UNRULY MOVE™
Choose Voice Over Visibility

When visibility and authenticity feel at odds, choose authenticity. Visibility built on performance is fragile. Voice? That's unshakable.

This is what it means to be unruly *and lead*. Not just in theory. In public. In real time. Even on LinkedIn.

CHAPTER SEVEN:
Limits and Leverage

You feel the spark.
Then the stop.
The pull to say it,
followed by the freeze.
Like a hand on your chest,
holding you back.
And you don't know why.
You just know:
Not allowed.

When Mark, the CEO, called me late on a Friday, his voice was tight, like someone trying not to splinter. Trying to sound composed. But underneath, the panic was bleeding through.

"We keep losing people," he said. "Our culture used to be electric. Now it feels like everyone is walking on eggshells. No one's saying anything, but you can feel it. Something's wrong."

He was right.

When I stepped into the organization, the tension was unmistakable. People kept their heads down. Collaboration felt forced. Meetings were short and stiff. The life force had drained out of the place.

It didn't take long to find the source: *David.*

David was a senior leader and high performer, responsible for nearly half the company's revenue. On paper, he looked like an asset. But, in reality, he was leaving emotional wreckage in his wake.

He cut people off mid-sentence. Took credit for work that wasn't his. Dominated conversations. Made team members feel small and unsure of themselves.

The damage wasn't immediate. It built like rust. Quiet. Corrosive.
Just under the surface.

Engagement dropped. Innovation slowed. And eventually, people just stopped showing up—physically or mentally. The culture was eroding from the inside out.

So, I went back to Mark. Told him what I saw.

Mark already knew. He'd known for a while.

But knowing isn't the same as acting. And for months, he had done what many leaders do when faced with a powerful performer who's causing quiet damage:

He hoped the problem would fix itself. He downplayed the string of resignations. He focused on financial success to distract from the human toll. He rationalized David's behavior to others and to himself.

He told himself that David's value outweighed the disruption. That confrontation might backfire. That the team was just adjusting. That the culture would course-correct on its own.

But underneath all that logic was fear. Fear of the fallout. Fear of being wrong. Fear of admitting he'd defended someone who was quietly breaking everything.

And guilt. The kind that simmers when you realize you've been prioritizing the wrong things.

What made it harder? He wasn't the only one who saw it.

Elena, the COO, had been sounding the alarm for months. She's the kind of leader who sees the cracks before they collapse the structure. The one who names the discomfort in the room, even when it's easier not to. She saw the dip in morale. She saw the exodus of quiet talent. She saw David's behavior and its ripple effect.

And, she had told Mark. Clearly. Repeatedly.

But Mark didn't act. Not because he didn't care but because he couldn't reconcile the truth she was naming with the rules he still believed: "We need that specific revenue to survive." "We can't afford to lose him."

Elena, spot on. But her insights, like so many offered by those not in the ultimate seat of power, were filed under "concerns" instead of "calls to action."

She wasn't angry. She was tired, the kind of tired that settles in your shoulders and makes your voice quieter. That wears you down not with hours, but with invisibility. And worse, she began to question her own value. When your clarity gets dismissed long enough, it doesn't just make you quiet. It makes you doubt whether your voice matters at all. Her confidence began to erode. *If speaking up didn't change anything, why bother?*

Elena is not just a character in this story. She's an avatar for every leader who sees the problem but can't make the call. For every voice of clarity that's been sidelined in favor of comfort. For the person reading this right now, who's been biting their tongue and questioning their gut.

You're not wrong.
You're just ahead of the curve.

THE RULE BEHIND THE SILENCE

That's when Mark said it: "I think it might be too late. We can't keep people. Everyone's tense. But we just . . . we can't lose David."

Not because of a contract. Not because of policy. Because of a rule they had never named, one that had embedded itself so deeply into the culture that it felt like fact: "Revenue matters more than culture."

And it's not just this company. It's everywhere.
One of the most quietly corrosive beliefs in modern leadership.

Not that culture and revenue are at odds, because they're not.
You *need* both.

But the belief that any one person is too valuable to hold accountable?
That the numbers will fall apart if you disrupt the status quo?
That keeping the peace is more important than protecting the culture?

That's not strategy.

It's fear and lack dressed up as pragmatism.
Polished, approved, and too afraid to challenge what's toxic.

And let's be honest:
Fear will always protect short-term comfort over long-term impact.

Refusing to do the hard thing because one person is seen as too precious to fire?
It's tanked more companies than I can count.

NOTICING IS THE FIRST ACT OF REBELLION

When I brought the team together, I wrote that sentence on a whiteboard: "Revenue matters more than culture."

And then I asked them: What limits are guiding you?

Where did they come from? Are they true?

The room cracked open. The CFO confessed to having a special "David budget" for unpredictable demands. HR had rewritten policies just to manage him. A new leader said she'd been warned not to challenge him directly—it was just "how things worked."

Three weeks later, they did what they thought was impossible. They let him go. And the organization exhaled.

It wasn't clean. It wasn't easy. But it was exactly what needed to be done.

Mark told me later, "We thought we couldn't afford to lose him. What we couldn't afford was another day of pretending this wasn't breaking us."

WHAT LOOKS LIKE STRATEGY MIGHT BE FEAR

That's the thing about limits: They don't just block your growth; they start to reshape how you see yourself. They show up in your language, your leadership, even your nervous system. They masquerade as strategy, humility, and loyalty. And they always make sense . . . until they don't.

Like when you keep a toxic high performer on the team because "we need their revenue," even though morale is crashing. Or when you delay a hard conversation in the name of harmony, but it's really avoidance. Or when you bury your real vision under bullet points and call it strategy.

We all have our limits; some we inherited, some we built ourselves. And some of the most painful moments in leadership come from realizing we've let those limits define us.

But here's something even more infuriating: seeing someone else do the thing we told ourselves we couldn't.

The product you dreamed up but shelved, maybe because you thought it wasn't the right time, or feared no one would take it seriously, only to watch someone else launch it and win. The boundary you never set, because you were afraid of being seen as difficult, while someone else drew their line and gained more respect. The version of leadership you secretly crave—more human, more bold, more free—that you keep deferring until it's "safe," while someone else makes it their calling card and gets promoted for it.

That's how limits work. Quietly. Logically. Until you realize they're not keeping you safe. They're keeping you small, like walls that were meant to shelter you but now block the view. At first, they protect. Eventually, they imprison.

And the truth is, you'll never feel entirely right in a life that was built by obeying the wrong rules.

UNSPOKEN LIMITS, VISIBLE COSTS

According to a 2022 MIT Sloan study, toxic culture is the number one predictor of employee attrition: ten times more powerful than compensation. And one of the fastest ways a culture turns toxic? *Letting unchallenged rules dictate reality.*

NOT JUST STORIES. BLUEPRINTS.

They didn't start with power. They started with something else: a refusal to obey rules that no longer made sense. A quiet no to the assumptions that didn't fit. A deep inner conviction that the impossible wasn't a reason to quit, it was a reason to start.

Sara Blakely didn't have fashion credentials. She was selling fax machines door-to-door when she cut the feet off her pantyhose and pitched a billion-dollar idea. Everyone told her no. Wrong time, wrong industry, no experience. She launched **SPANX**® anyway and changed the game for women everywhere.

Antoni Gaudí barely graduated from architecture school, then redefined it. Inspired by bones and trees more than bricks and blueprints, he built flowing structures that seemed to sprout from the earth. People thought he was mad. Today, **LA SAGRADA FAMÍLIA** is one of the most visited sites in the world.

Julia Vitarello had no medical background. But when her daughter Mila was diagnosed with a fatal, rare disease, she co-developed the first-ever patient-customized drug, changing the future of medicine. One mother. One fight. One line she refused to accept. Today, the "Mila to Millions" campaign continues to push for individualized treatment for rare diseases.

They weren't rebels. They were clear.

Their defiance wasn't noise, it was direction. It wasn't chaos, it was clarity.

THE LIMITS YOU CAN'T SEE ARE THE ONES RUNNING YOU

Some limits are internal. You learned them early. Like: "Don't outshine your mentor." "Wait until you're sure." "Play nice."

Others are cultural. You absorbed them in systems and workplaces. Like: "That's not how we do things here." "Be realistic." "Stay in your lane."

Both kinds share one goal: to keep you safe. But they often do the opposite. They shrink you. Quiet you. Dim the thing that made you powerful in the first place.

UNRULY CHALLENGE™
Identify Your Limits

Take a moment to name a rule you've been living by, one that feels constraining or outdated.

Write it down, in its rawest form. Don't make it pretty. Make it honest.

1. Where did it come from?
2. Who taught it to you?
3. What is it trying to protect?
4. Most importantly, what is it costing you?

This is where Strategic Unruliness™ starts to sharpen: with the courage to name what no longer fits. *You don't have to dismantle everything overnight. But you do have to start telling the truth.*

UNRULY MOVE™
Name It

Name the rule that's been quietly running the show.

Interlude
TERABITHIA WASN'T JUST A FORT

Terabithia was my refuge.

A hidden world built from branches and books and fierce imagination.

I named it after the one in the novel, *Bridge to Terabithia*—because even back then, I knew magic and grief could live in the same place.

It wasn't just play.

It was survival.

I wasn't hiding from monsters.

I was hiding from the slow ache of being misunderstood. From the weight of always performing. From the feeling that even when I was winning, I was still alone.

In Terabithia, I could be the queen. The hero. The rule-maker.

It was the first space I claimed that was fully mine. Not for approval. Not for applause. Not even for safety. Just for me.

That fort taught me what so many leaders forget:

Your clearest vision starts in the places no one else sees.

Defend your inner world.

Build from there.

And if you haven't found your Terabithia yet, start small. Create one space where you get to tell the truth, make the rules, and lead from your gut.

That's where your clarity lives.
That's where you find your limit.
That's how you start to lead on your terms.

Find your Terabithia.

CHAPTER EIGHT:

The Day That Shifted Everything

It feels certain. Like breath returning. Like space opening.
This rule isn't mine. And just like that—you are free.

The competition was less than an hour away, and I hadn't moved. My body felt like stone—breath shallow, limbs heavy, a dull buzz in my ears that made everything feel distant. It wasn't nerves. It was knowing. A bone-deep signal I'd never felt in a competition before: I didn't want to dance. I was frozen, wrapped in a hotel towel on the edge of a sagging bed, heart pounding but hollow, staring at a rack of rhinestone-covered costumes like they held the answer. My muscles ached from three days of battle rounds, my ribs still tender from my partner catching me in a trick over and over through so many rounds, but none of that compared to the dull ache in my chest, the one that whispered, "This isn't it anymore."

It was November. Hyatt Regency, Columbus, Ohio. Same weekend as the Michigan vs. Ohio State football game. Drunk football fans stumbled in as the bars closed. Meanwhile, we were just leaving the ballroom at 2 a.m., having fought round after round, hoping to dance our way into the finals.

I'd survived three days of intense preliminary competition. And now, I was sitting on a brown and yellow bedspread in a dated, dingy hotel room, staring at a rack of glittering dresses. Thinking about everything I'd sacrificed to get here. The time. The money. The weekends away from my family. The sore muscles. The broken ribs.

And for the first time in my life, I didn't want to dance. Not because I didn't love it, but because I couldn't feel it anymore. The fire was gone. The joy had faded. All I could feel was the pressure to perform: to smile, sparkle, and squeeze myself into a version of success that no longer felt like mine.

Not because I was afraid of losing. I'd lost before. But because I suddenly couldn't stomach the thought of walking into another ballroom pretending to be someone I no longer wanted to be.

I looked at the dress I was supposed to wear. It was beautiful. Hand-sewn. It shimmered in all the right ways. And I felt nothing. No connection. No joy. Just weight.

This was supposed to be my year to win. After seven years of competing, this was the one everyone said would be mine.

And the thought came. Quiet, almost absurd:

What if I didn't?

What if I didn't wear the dress? What if I didn't style my hair into the tight, polished twist everyone expected? What if I didn't force myself to play the part one more time?

What if I just showed up as me?

I didn't have a plan. I had a feeling—a clear, full-body knowing that couldn't be charted on paper but was pulsing with direction. Sometimes, that's where the real transformation begins.

So, I threw on a sweatshirt and walked downstairs to the sponsor booth—not to buy, but to ask. I was sponsored. My designer supplied my dresses. But that evening, I didn't want any of them. I perused the racks, looking for something, although I had no idea what.

Then I saw it, tucked behind a row of show costumes, not competition pieces. *A catsuit.* Sleek. No skirt. Not what anyone wore to compete. I knew instantly: That's it.

It was midnight blue. Full-length. Sheer lace from shoulder to ankle—bold but elegant. The halter neckline plunged into a deep V, edged in silver rhinestones that caught the light with every turn. A wide, white crystal belt wrapped around the waist, drawing the eye and commanding attention. It didn't flow. It didn't spin. It sculpted. No skirt to swirl. No fringe to flutter. Just unapologetic presence.

I asked if I could wear it.

Donna blinked. She had been making my costumes for years, and wasn't just my sponsor, but my friend. "Babygirl, that's not a competition piece." Her words were pointed, and her voice held a flicker of judgment, the kind that says, "You're about to throw something important away." But I'd already thrown away the illusion that playing by their rules would lead to joy. What she saw as recklessness, I knew was reclamation.

"It was worn in a show. You can't wear that. You can't compete in a catsuit."

I didn't back down. I told her I wasn't going out there in anything else.

She sighed. "It's your year to win. You are going to lose if you wear that."

The room thickened, like the air itself recoiled. Her words didn't shout, but they landed with a finality that stretched the silence, daring me to second-guess myself.

I didn't care.

She just shook her head at me. Disapproval all over her face. But she handed it over.

"Fine," she said. "It's your funeral, girlfriend."

Back upstairs, I pulled it on. Did my own makeup. Left my hair half-down—soft, loose, exactly the way I liked it. When I looked in the mirror, I didn't see a rule-breaker. I saw a goddess. Powerful. Fierce. Not traditional, maybe. But fully aligned. I didn't look like a typical ballroom dancer. I looked like the boldest version of me.

And I danced.

I danced with a fire I forgot I possessed. Playing with the audience, inviting them into each dance with the full force of my presence—letting them feel every moment by amplifying how I moved, what I felt, what I knew through every part of my body—from my feet to my fingertips. So immersed in the dancing, I totally forgot there were nine judges or anyone else on the floor. It was me, my partner, and the audience. *In perfect sync.*

I danced for the win. But this time, on my terms. With my body, my rhythm, my voice. I wasn't trying to impress anyone—but I was there to take up space. Fully. Fiercely. As myself.

I danced the way I used to before I knew what winning looked like. I danced like someone who had finally stopped auditioning for belonging.

And . . . I lost. Badly.

The judges weren't subtle. My coaches were furious. "What were you thinking?" one asked, exasperated.

But for the first time, I wasn't ashamed. I was free.

I didn't know how to explain it yet. I just knew I couldn't go back.

So, I didn't.

I kept showing up in catsuits. Kept dancing like myself, for myself. And for a while, I kept losing.

But something had shifted. I was alive again.

And then one day, the results changed. I started winning. Not because I'd contorted into something more acceptable. But because I had become undeniable.

And soon, other dancers started showing up in catsuits too. Within a year, I looked around the dance floor and saw them everywhere—bold, sleek, unapologetic. What was once unthinkable had become a trend. Because one act of truth can ignite a thousand acts of courage. Break the rule—and you become proof that freedom is possible.

They didn't ask for permission either. They just stepped into the space I made—and made it their own.

What started as a quiet refusal became an invitation—not just to break a rule, but to reimagine what was possible. One act of courage shifted the atmosphere, showing everyone in that ballroom—and beyond—that change doesn't need permission. It just needs a spark.

This wasn't about rebellion. It was about truth—the kind that isn't polished or palatable, but personal and precise. Truth, in this context, means owning what's real for you—even when it breaks the mold, disrupts expectations, or makes people uncomfortable.

Truth isn't about being right. It's about being real.

The most unruly thing you can do isn't break the rule. *It is believing in yourself before anyone else does.*

That was the first time I understood what it meant to be strategically unruly. Not reactive. Not defiant for the sake of drama.

But clear. Intentional. Whole.

It didn't just change how I danced. It changed how I lead.

Because when you challenge the rules that no longer fit—you don't just make space for yourself. You create space for everyone else to stop performing too.

Sometimes the rule isn't about sequins or silence—it's about shrinking your brilliance, so others don't feel threatened.

So let me ask you: What rule are you ready to kick to the curb?

Not someday. Not when it's safe. Now.

UNRULY CHALLENGE™
Challenge a Rule

Think of a rule you've been living by—one that feels familiar but limiting. It might be about how you show up. What you're allowed to say. What you believe is required to be taken seriously. Now ask:

1. Was this rule made for you?
2. Was it made for this moment?
3. Is it helping you (and your people) thrive?

If the answer to any of those is no—challenge it. In mindset. In action. In conversation. You don't have to blow it all up. Just take the next bold, honest step. Your catsuit moment is waiting.

Because the longer you follow a rule that was never made for you, the more distant your real power becomes.

UNRULY MOVE™
Unlock New Space

Ask the questions that unlock new space. Example: "You can't change your mind as a leader." Or: "Bold colors don't belong in the boardroom." What's one rule like that you're ready to question?

And if you've already broken one—what space did it create?

Interlude
DID THE OTHER LAWYER SHOW UP?

I was the youngest litigator in my firm to take a case to trial. I won.

The senior partner walked into my office afterward, smirking.
"Did the lawyer on the other side even show up?"

It was meant as a joke.

But what it revealed was the rule: If I won, it had to be luck. Or softness from the opponent. Or a fluke.

Because if it were skill—real, commanding, courtroom skill—that would disrupt the entire hierarchy. Women aren't supposed to win without explanation. And if they do, it better come with a punchline.

I didn't laugh. I just looked at him and said, "Yeah. He showed up. He just lost."

He didn't ask again.

But the rule stayed in the air for years: Don't be better. Don't be obvious. Don't make the men uncomfortable.

Break the rule. Win anyway.

What rule is ready to go next?

- And get ready—because next, we're not just going to challenge the rules. We're going to rewrite them.

PART III:
The Rebuild

CHAPTER NINE:

The Power of Integration

For the first time, it feels easy. And you realize—it was never supposed to be that hard.

Jesse Cole and his wife bought a crumbling baseball stadium in Savannah, Georgia. The roof leaked. The paint peeled. The bleachers groaned with every step. Their team? A failing minor league group that couldn't draw a crowd even with free beer. And when they opened their first season? They sold three season tickets.

Three.

It wasn't just humbling—it was humiliating. They drained their savings, slept on an air mattress that deflated in the night, and clung to a dream the world mocked—their backs sore, their hearts stretched thin, and their belief pressed under the weight of every 'no' they refused to accept.

But Jesse had a vision.

He didn't want just to make baseball joyful. He tried to make it unforgettable. A fusion of circus, theater, and sport. A full body YES for fans who never felt invited into the game.

He got clear on his objective: Make baseball irresistible—not just for purists, but for families, kids, skeptics. He didn't tweak baseball. He reimagined it.

He found the limits—rules that had calcified into culture:

- Games with no time limits
- Long stretches of dead air
- Players discouraged from fan interaction
- Rigid roles: Cheerleaders had to look and act a certain way
- No music. No dancing. No fun.

Then he challenged them: Was this made for us? Was it made for this moment? Does it help us thrive?

No. No. And absolutely not.

So, he eliminated the noise and made space for something new.

Timed games. Dancing players. No mound visits. Breakdancing coaches. A pep band in the stands. Banana Nanas shaking the bleachers. Players delivering roses to fans. Every tradition became a question—and an opportunity. One moment, fans sat quietly in their seats. The next, they were tossing popcorn in time with the music, laughing at choreographed pitcher dances, cheering as players leapt into the stands with roses. The game wasn't just watched—it was felt. It was unforgettable.

He didn't ask: What's allowed? He asked: What's possible?

That's Strategic Unruliness™ in action.

He didn't use this framework—but if he had, here's what it would've looked like:

1. Find the limits—Identify what's stale, inherited, or quietly suffocating the vision.
2. Challenge the rules—Ask: Was this made for us? For now? Is it helping us thrive?
3. Expand capacity—Clear the noise. Reclaim the full spectrum. Build something bigger.

Jesse didn't just disrupt. He expanded. He didn't just entertain. He awakened. He stopped performing someone else's version of leadership—and brought all of himself to the table.

There was resistance. Ridicule. Financial panic. Doubt from every corner. But he held.

Now? Sold-out stadiums. National media. Half a million people on a waitlist. Families flying cross-country to catch a Savannah Banana's game.

He didn't just build a team. He built a movement.

That's what Strategic Unruliness™ makes possible.

I once asked a group of brilliant leaders: If I handed you the perfect strategy for your biggest challenge—would you have the capacity to implement it?

Seventy-six percent said no.

Not because they doubted the solution. Because they were carrying too much of what no longer fit—over-functioning, outdated roles, identity edits they didn't know they were making.

We've been trained to slice ourselves up. Be the expert here. The strategist there. The human—only in small, approved doses.

Every self-edit drains your power.

This isn't just burnout. It's identity fatigue.

Strategic Unruliness™ doesn't just ask what you're challenging—it asks: What part of yourself have you been hiding? And what might become possible if you stopped?

Take Elena. The COO I told you about, who worked with Mark. She held the culture together like scaffolding. Measured. Steady. But inside, she saw the truth—and it was wrecking her. She wasn't tired from the workload. She was tired from holding her truth behind her teeth—from the constant pressure to calibrate, translate, and soften what she knew for the comfort of others.

The day she stopped filtering? Everything shifted. She didn't get louder. She got truer.

That's the move. Reclamation. Not reinvention.

Same for Horacio Pagani. Lamborghini told him: Stay in your lane. You're a designer.

But he wasn't just a designer. He was a sculptor, engineer, and visionary. He didn't want to build cars. He wanted to create moving poetry.

They told him to stick to sketches. He built a lab. Created machines that made people weep.

The Zonda R wasn't a product. It was a rebuke to small thinking. Because Pagani brought his whole self to the table.

You've seen this before:

- Steve Jobs and calligraphy. A class taken out of curiosity—no business logic. But it gave birth to the Macintosh's revolutionary typography. Fonts that weren't just readable—they were beautiful. He didn't compartmentalize art and tech. He fused them to create a product the world had never seen. And that fusion became the industry standard. His integration expanded the capacity of an entire field.

- Lin-Manuel Miranda and *Hamilton*. A fusion of rap, history, and heritage. He didn't soften it to fit Broadway. He rewrote what Broadway could be—gave voice to a new kind of storytelling and brought people into the theater who had never felt represented. His boldness sparked a wave of new creators who saw that their stories, too, belonged on stage.

- Yvon Chouinard and Patagonia®. A climber who turned capitalism into activism. Giving away the company wasn't a PR move—it was a radical statement of values. His commitment to the earth became the company's core engine, rewriting what business could look like. His stand reshaped what generations of founders now believe is possible.

These weren't side interests. They were integrations. They didn't ask, "Does this part belong?" They declared, "This is me."

The same thing happened with my clients: Erica, a corporate controller who sketched logos for fun. When the marketing team hit a wall during a rebrand, she hesitated, then shared one of her designs. It wasn't just good—it was electric. It broke the brief and set the tone for the whole campaign. Suddenly, she wasn't just the numbers person. She was the spark. Her creativity didn't just change the logo—it shifted how the team saw her, and how she saw herself. The walls between roles cracked open. That sketch became the company's new brand. Not a hobby. A hidden superpower. And it didn't stop with her. That one moment of courage triggered a cultural unlock: What else—and who else—have we been overlooking?

Jared—a real estate exec obsessed with luxury. He kept his existing business model humming, but inside, he was craving more. For years, he believed he had to choose—between staying with the tried-and-true model or abandoning it to chase a different vision. But the answer wasn't either/or. It was AND. He carved out space for a new experiment—a luxury retail vertical that no one on his team believed would work. He built it quietly, almost like a startup inside the firm. Within months, it began to outpace expectations. Within a year, it surpassed the original portfolio in both revenue and buzz. Investors took notice. His team saw a different side of him—visionary, risk-tolerant, and alive. He didn't switch paths. He widened the lane. And in doing so, his whole organization grew.

They didn't reinvent. They reintegrated. And when they did, their capacity exploded.

UNRULY CHALLENGE™
Hidden Capacity Scan

Ask yourself:

- What do I love that I've told myself doesn't belong here?
- What strengths do others admire that I downplay?
- Where do I feel most like myself—and what would it look like to lead from there?

Pick one. Bring it into a room where you usually would edit it out. Watch what changes.

UNRULY MOVE™
Reclaim It

Reclaim the part of you that expands the whole.

Interlude
JUST DON'T DANCE

No one said it out loud—not directly. But I heard it in every sideways glance. Every polite nod. Every "Wow, I didn't know you danced."

Don't be too expressive. Don't be too free. Don't be too much.

You're a lawyer. A mother. A wife. You can dance—but don't let anyone know you dance.

And if you do it? Do it quietly. Appropriately. Don't enjoy it too much. Don't move your hips like that. Don't wear that costume. Don't post that video.

People asked, "Your husband lets you dance with another man?" "You leave your kids to go compete?" "What do your colleagues think about this?"

For years, I danced in secret. In dim studios, after hours, off the grid.

Even then, I held back. I moved, but I didn't express myself fully. I showed up, but not all the way. I was always one glance, one gesture, one costume choice away from being misunderstood—or worse, discredited.

Because joy, sensuality, full-body freedom? They didn't fit the version of success I thought would keep me safe.

They weren't part of the script.
Not for a serious, professional woman. A wife. A mother.
Not for someone who wanted to be taken seriously in rooms where power looked a certain way.

So, I danced—but I also apologized.

Until one day, I didn't.

I danced like I meant it. Like my joy was just as sacred as my strategy. Like I wasn't going to split myself anymore.

And when I did? Everything changed.

Not because I became someone new. But because I finally stopped hiding who I already was.

Dancing was never the problem. Hiding was. Not the kind of hiding that you do in shadows—the kind you do in plain sight, dressed in a navy blazer, cloaked in credentials, all while shrinking from your own fire.

And the rule? It was never about movement.

It was about power.

Break the rule. Dance anyway.

CHAPTER TEN:

Power That Starts in Your Feet

It starts in your feet.
Solid. Certain. Unshaken.
You're not trying to fit.
You know you belong.
You have a secret weapon no one told you about.
And you're about to unlock it.

When I walked into the boardroom for my first executive team meeting, every eye tracked me like a spotlight. I was the new Director of Leadership and Development. It was a newly created role. *And only the Dean wanted me there.*

This wasn't a blank slate. This was a legacy table—a leadership team loyal to the old guard, with unspoken hierarchies and deeply set dynamics.

People smiled. Politely. But their posture said it all: *Who let you in?*

I felt it in my chest first—the squeeze of doubt, the weight of expectation, the voice that whispered, *You don't belong here.*

For a split second, the swirl threatened to overtake me. Every instinct said prove yourself. Posture. Impress.

But I didn't.

I grounded.
Paused.
Pressed my feet into the floor.
Felt the soles connect, like roots remembering the ground.
Imagined a zipper running from my feet up the center of my body—and zipped myself up, slow and steady.
Shoulders rolled back and down.
Spine stacked.
Chin lifted. Eyes focused—with just a hint of humor.
And then I exhaled.

Not performative. Not defensive.
Just present.

The nerves didn't vanish—but they quieted. My body led, and my mind followed. My nervous system steadied. *You earned this seat.*

When I spoke, I didn't overexplain or overcompensate. I asked a bold, strategic question that reframed the meeting.
Heads turned. Pens paused.
Not because I demanded the room—but because I claimed it.

That's Body Power™.

Before you say a word, your body speaks.

We think power lives in ideas. In polish. In presence.
But real power starts deeper than that—it begins in your body.

Body Power™ is the secret weapon most leaders don't know they need. But once you unlock it, you never lead the same way again.
This isn't extra. It's everything.

Another time, I watched a room misread power in real time.

A man walked in, tentative. He paused two feet into the doorway, scanning for an open seat. The room was almost full. He hesitated, uncertain. People looked up, then quickly dismissed him. No one knew who he was—and his body said he wasn't important.

Then a woman entered. Confident. Clear. She paused, smiled, walked directly to a seat, and greeted those around her with ease. Heads turned. Eyes lingered. Who is *she*?

He was the keynote speaker from New York.
She was the newest sales rep, sent because no one else could make it.

He had authority. But she had the presence.

And presence always walks in first.

This is embodied leadership.
Not performance. Practice.
When you ground your body, you change your brain. Shift your chemistry. Rewrite the story—not with affirmations, but with presence.

What they call confidence is often just embodied clarity. The kind that doesn't ask for permission.

Forget what you were taught about "professionalism." Authentic leadership doesn't shrink.

This chapter is about posture. But not the way you've been taught. This is posture as power. As presence. As strategy.

You may have heard of power posing—great for a quick hit. But it fades. Power Posture™, on the other hand, sustains. As long as your body holds the position, your nervous system stays grounded, and your voice carries weight.

It's not a gimmick. It's physiology.

So, when you enter a room, zip up from the floor:

POWER POSTURE™ WALKTHROUGH

- Start at your feet. Press them firmly into the ground.
- Imagine a zipper running up the centerline of your body. Zip yourself up, slow and strong.
- Stack your spine. Roll your shoulders back and drop them.
- Lift your chin. Focus your eyes with intention and ease.
- Exhale. And keep breathing.

You should feel tall, calm, and *ready*.

ASK YOURSELF:

- What message is my body sending right now?
- Am I grounded—or guarding?
- Where do I feel tension, and what's it trying to protect?
- What would it feel like to stand like I already belong here?

Move in this posture. Breathe. Shift your weight. Let your body lead.

PRO TIP: DON'T LOCK YOUR KNEES.
KEEP A MICRO-BEND. THINK ROOTED, NOT RIGID.

Your body holds memory—of shrinking, surviving, performing. But it also, holds the power to lead from your center.

You don't need to fake confidence. You need to *inhabit* it.

Because when your body believes you? Your mind follows.

UNRULY CHALLENGE™
Embody the Message

Before your next high-stakes moment:

1. Ground your feet. Press them onto the floor like roots.
2. Zip up from the floor.
3. Shoulders back. Chin lifted.
4. Eyes calm and clear. Let a knowing smile play.
5. Exhale fully.

Then walk in like the room is already yours. Let your body speak first.

UNRULY MOVE™
Lead from the Ground Up

Pick one moment this week to shift your power—not with words, but with presence.
Stand tall. Breathe deep. Move like you mean it.
Because your body knows what your mind forgets:

You're already enough.
And you're ready now.

Interlude
THE DARE

The restaurant was packed. Loud. Slow service. But we didn't care. It gave us time to play our favorite game: decoding the dynamics of every couple in the room.

"Bad first date," I whispered to Mia, nodding toward the awkward pair one table over.

"How do you know?"

"Look at her posture," I said. "Straight-backed, arms crossed, eyes darting. She's planning her escape."

Sure enough, the guy was leaning in, talking nonstop, oblivious. The more he talked, the more she recoiled.

Moments later, she bolted to the bathroom.

We followed.

Inside, she was already on the phone. "Get me out of here. This guy is a nightmare. Bragging nonstop. Doesn't care what I think. I'm done."

We offered backup. She sighed, collected herself, and walked back out.

"You totally called it," Mia said.

"Body language never lies," I told her. "We leak truth. But here's the thing most people miss: We can shift it. On purpose. With presence."

"Like how?"

"Like turning every head in this restaurant. Want to try? I dare you."

Mia laughed. "Dare accepted."

We got to work.

"Stand tall. Push your feet onto the floor. Zip yourself up. Shoulders back. Chest open. Head high. Breathe. Eyes forward. Walk like you own it. Slowly. Don't rush. Feel every step."

And she did.

Mia walked out like she was royalty. Not flashy. Just grounded. Intentional. Eyes up. Energy contained but undeniable.

Heads turned. Conversations paused.

When she reached the table, she collapsed into her chair, wide-eyed. "Did that really just happen?"

"Yes," I grinned. "And you can do it anytime."

Presence is power. It doesn't require noise or performance. Just clarity. Embodied.

You don't have to wait for permission to own the room. Just dare to take up space.

CHAPTER ELEVEN:

Leading Without Applause

You take the breath.
The one that comes after truth.
You wait for the reaction —
but nothing comes.
Still,
your body knows:
You did the right thing.
And this time,
that's enough.

Maya closed her laptop slowly.

She'd finished unveiling the new initiative—the one that had kept her up for weeks, the one built from her deepest clarity. It wasn't just a strategic pivot. It was a statement: We don't have to lead like this anymore.

She'd stood in front of her team, heart open, voice steady, and told the truth. About the work. About what was no longer working. About what she believed they could build together.

She was braced for electricity. For the swell of energy that comes when a room leans in.

She got polite nods. A few questions. Mostly positive responses.
And then, silence.

They moved on.

No one pushed back. But no one leaned in either.

She sat in her office now, the quiet now louder than any criticism.

This was supposed to be the moment. The rally cry. The ignition point. Instead, it felt like a whisper into the void.

Was it too much? Too soon? Did I misread the room?

She expected fireworks. She got crickets.

And if you've never seen yourself reflected in the rooms you lead—that silence can feel even louder.

For some of us, applause was never promised.
We were taught to earn our place, to prove our value, to soften our tone. So when the room doesn't cheer, it doesn't just sting. It threatens to confirm every old story about being too much, too different, not enough.

This wasn't resistance. This was something more subtle. More disorienting. The emotional whiplash that comes after you do the brave thing—and the world doesn't know what to do with it.

She had changed. But the system hadn't caught up yet.

She closed the laptop again. But this time, it wasn't silence she heard—it was her own conviction. Quiet, steady, and unshaken.

THE DISTINCTION NO ONE MAKES—
BUT YOU NEED TO HEAR

Most leadership books talk about resistance—and they should.

Resistance is real. It's the inner backlash, the societal pushback, the fear of being too much, too fast, too bold. It's the moment you feel the edge of your limits—and everything in you tightens.

But there's another moment no one talks about:
The silence after the clarity.

You made the move. Said the thing. Quit the game. Named your truth.

And then . . . it got quiet.

This isn't resistance. This is the aftermath.

Resistance is the fear of what might happen if you break the rules. Aftermath is what actually happens when you do.

One is the storm before the shift.
The other is the silence after the thunder.

Most people assume the shift itself is the peak—the bold conversation, the big leap, the clean break. But any real transformation has two parts:

The breaking.
And the becoming.

And the becoming is quiet.

That's what this chapter is about.

What it feels like to walk into the new world you just claimed—and realize you still have to build it, brick by brick, without applause, without a map, and sometimes . . . without company.

But this isn't failure.

This is the building phase—the often-overlooked stretch of time where clarity becomes culture, and ideas become structure. It's not glamorous. It's not fast. But it's the part where your vision gets roots.

And it's where your real opportunity to build what's next begins.

And here is the thing: Every time you hold your ground in that silence—

You widen the path for someone else to show up unedited.

You're not just breaking patterns. You're rewriting what leadership looks like.

THE LETDOWN AFTER THE LEAP

They told you to trust yourself. To speak up. To make the move.

So, you did.

And now, you're in the middle of your new life and wondering why it still feels shaky.

This is the whiplash of growth. The emotional hangover of clarity. You did the bold thing, and instead of feeling free and affirmed, you now feel exposed and alone.

Here's what no one tells you: *Expansion doesn't feel like a high. It often feels like grief.*

You're grieving old identities. Old certainties. Old safety.

Even if the old world was too small—it was familiar. And humans crave familiarity, even when it hurts us.

This isn't you regressing. This is you recalibrating.

You're no longer who you were. But you're not yet who you're becoming.

That gap? It's not a failure. It's the forge. And it's also the reason most people won't do this work.

Because it's not glamorous, it's not fast. And it's often unpopular, at least at first.

Sitting with the discomfort—and sometimes, the emptiness—is the hardest part because there's no applause here. No instant reward. Just you, your vision, and the quiet work of becoming.

This is why most people backtrack. They confuse the discomfort of expansion with the comfort of certainty. They retreat into clarity's shadow instead of holding their ground.

But if you can stay . . . if you can let yourself be with the uncertainty without abandoning the truth you found . . .

That's where *the build* begins.

Stay there. Breathe through it. Don't make it mean something's wrong.

You're not doing it wrong. You're just doing something real.

THE LONELINESS OF THE UNRULY LEADER

You've crossed the threshold. You've said the true thing. You've chosen clarity over comfort.

And suddenly, it's quiet. This is the part where people don't rush to affirm you. They hesitate. They need time. They're recalibrating too—not because you were wrong, but because you're no longer predictable.

Clarity shifts power. And when power shifts, people get uncomfortable.

They're used to the version of you who smoothed edges, played translator, filled gaps. The one who made things palatable. The one who led from accommodation, not activation.

But now? You're showing up without the softeners. You're not asking for permission. You're not managing their comfort.

And that can feel threatening—not because you're being harmful, but because you're being honest.

This is when it gets lonely. Not because you're alone, but because you're ahead. When you lead with vision, you stop belonging to the crowd. You belong to the future.

And the future is a lonely place at first.

You will question yourself. You will want to take it back. You will miss the ease of fitting in—even if it never fed you.

But here's the truth: You're not crazy. You're not broken. You're not alone. You're just ahead.

And your clarity—though it costs you comfort—is creating space.

Not everyone will join you. But the right ones will find you.

Stay unruly.

WAIT—ISN'T THIS RESISTANCE?

Let's name it clearly: What Maya's feeling right now is not resistance. It's aftermath.

And that distinction matters.

Resistance is the pushback that shows up when you're about to change. It tries to keep you safe by keeping you small. It comes from inside you—and from the systems around you—to prevent disruption.

Aftermath is what shows up after you've already changed. It's the quiet, the doubt, the second-guessing. It's your system recalibrating to your new size—and the world taking a minute (or longer) to catch up.

Resistance says: "Don't do it. It's too risky."
Aftermath says: "You did it. Are you sure it was worth it?"

One tries to stop your expansion.

The other tests your commitment.

They're both part of the cycle. And they don't just happen once.

Every level of leadership brings both.

And understanding the difference? That's what keeps you moving—instead of mistaking your becoming for a mistake.

HOLDING THE VISION IN THE NOISE

Most people want guarantees. Proof. A track record of success before they make the move.

But leadership—*real leadership*—doesn't work that way.

Conviction is not contingent on consensus. And vision doesn't wait for evidence.

You don't get the data before the leap. You get it after, if you're lucky.

That's why this part is so hard.

You've made the bold move. But there's still no sign it worked. People are quiet. The system is adjusting. You're halfway across a bridge you had to build while walking it.

And part of you wants to run back.

Let me tell you about someone who didn't.

She wasn't famous. She wasn't established. She hadn't booked a single paid gig. But she knew she had something to say. A fire to light. A stage to take.

So, she spent over $50,000 building the brand, the website, the platform—not because the world asked for it, but because she was claiming it. Before the bookings. Before the recognition. Before a single standing ovation.

Was she scared? Absolutely.

But she also knew *if she waited for evidence, she'd never leap.*

She didn't need permission. She needed to move. And that decision—to act as if it were already true—created the truth.

The gigs came. The stage found her. The brand didn't make her a speaker—her conviction did.

Because conviction isn't about being sure it will work. It's about being sure it matters.

(And if you want proof it works on a bigger stage? Just ask Matthew McConaughey. He turned down every rom-com he was offered—millions of dollars—and sat with no work for over a year before **DALLAS BUYERS CLUB** landed in his lap. That role won him an Oscar. The wait paid off. But the conviction came first.)

They leapt without a net. Without applause. Without certainty.

Because conviction isn't about being sure it will work. It's about being sure it matters.

That's what Maya is building now. Not just a new strategy, but a new standard.

And this part? It's profoundly countercultural.

We're taught to chase certainty. To move when we know the ROI. To calculate every step, then act. But that's not how leadership—or transformation—works.

This isn't about hoping it works. This is about moving, whether it does or not.

Because the real leaders? They aren't obsessed with outcomes. They're devoted to alignment.

You leap not because it's safe—you leap because you know who you are, and you refuse to lead from anywhere else.

And the only way it becomes real is if she keeps holding the vision, even when the room is silent.

For Maya, the silence didn't last. She held the line—and her team started to rise to meet it. Today, they're not just on board. They're building something none of them could've imagined before she spoke it out loud.

UNRULY CHALLENGE™
Staying with the Silence

This moment is where most people flinch—but you won't.

Use these prompts to stay connected to your vision, even when the room is silent:

1. When you made your bold move, what reaction were you secretly hoping for?
2. What meaning are you assigning to the silence you're experiencing?
3. In this quiet stretch, what part of you feels most tempted to shrink or backtrack?
4. What old identities or roles are you grieving—even if you know they no longer fit?
5. Who do you become when no one claps?
6. What would it look like to stay in alignment without needing affirmation?
7. Finish this sentence: "Even if no one gets it yet, I will keep showing up because . . ."

This is your practice. Not to prove anything. Not to push through. But to stay rooted in what's true—even when no one is watching.

UNRULY MOVE™
Act Like It's Already True

This week, choose one bold action that reinforces your vision—even if no one else sees it yet.

Invest in the thing. Launch the offer. Write the truth. Make the hire. Cancel what's no longer aligned.

Don't wait for signs. Be the sign.

Move not because the outcome is guaranteed, but because your clarity is.

Lead like the future you're building is already real.

Because the moment you do?
It starts to be.

Interlude
THE ROOM WAS SILENT

He stood in front of the room, the vision laid bare.

The one he'd been building in pieces for months—held close, refined in the quiet, carried with care.

It was bold. A new direction. A break from what came before. He believed in it. Knew it in his bones.

But as the last slide faded and the lights rose, no one moved.
No smiles. No protests. Just stillness.

He scanned the room. Faces unreadable. The silence crawled.
His breath caught for a moment. Maybe they hated it. Maybe it missed.
Maybe he had.

But then something deeper steadied him.
He grounded his feet. Let the doubt pass through. And remembered *the clarity wasn't new. It was just first.*

So, he stayed.
He didn't over-explain. Didn't retreat. Didn't chase applause.
He returned to the vision—not for them, but for himself.

And then, quietly, it began.
One conversation. One question. One person leaning in.
The silence didn't mean no.
It meant new.

And new takes time.

So, he built.
And eventually, they saw it too.

CHAPTER TWELVE:

When Pushback Means You're Close

It pushes.
Old fear. Old noise.
But something in you holds.
Grounded. Certain.
You don't flinch.
You don't fold.
Not this time.

The first time I danced on a keynote stage, it wasn't what I planned.

My heart was thudding in my chest—not from nerves exactly, but from the raw exposure of stepping fully into a moment I hadn't rehearsed. My hands felt electric. My breath came in quick and shallow. I knew I was about to cross a line I couldn't uncross—and a part of me thrilled at it, even as another part wanted to bolt.

I was booked for a breakout session at an HR leadership conference—not a headline moment, just a solid spot to speak. But when the organizer mentioned they didn't have anyone to close out the day, I offered to step in. I said I could pull the whole experience together with a final message—one that ended in dance. I even offered to do it for free.

She was excited. The committee was too. They said it would be fun, unexpected—a powerful way to end the conference.

But here's what actually happened:

It was 4 p.m. on a Friday. The head of the HR organization took the stage to close the day. She thanked the sponsors, handed out awards, told everyone the bar was open, and then said, like an afterthought, "Oh, and Kim Bolourtchi is going to lead you in some salsa dancing. Should be fun."

And then she walked off.

Before I could say a word, people started leaving. Heading for the bar. Grabbing their coats. I was left standing on stage, echoing through the ballroom, begging people to "come back," "dance with me," "it'll be fun, I promise."

It wasn't just a flop. It was a gut-punch—the kind that tightens your throat, makes your vision blur, and glues your feet to the stage. I felt the heat rush to my face, the sting of humiliation creeping up my spine. My voice wavered. The room felt like it was receding, cavernous and far away, like I was performing on the wrong stage of the wrong life. A soul-rattling moment that echoed every whispered fear I had tried to outrun. That I was too much. That I didn't belong. That my way—the embodied, unruly, all-in way—would never be taken seriously. It felt like every neon EXIT sign in the room was screaming: "Told you so."

And all I could think about was the advice I had heard over and over from the experts: "Don't do it."

They weren't being cruel. They were trying to protect me from moments like this.

And for a while, I let them.

But here's the cost: Even when the talk went well—even when I nailed the delivery, hit the laughter lines, landed the close—something always felt missing. Like I didn't really say what I came to say. Like I'd left my full self just offstage.

But something in me refused to die. Even when the stage rejected me, I knew—this wasn't about dance. It was about truth.

That moment didn't stop me. It sharpened me. Because even though it flopped—it taught me the one thing the experts never said:

You can't build a message about courage and lead from fear.

Eventually, I broke the format. I danced—not out of rebellion, but out of necessity. I remembered how the old format felt: perfectly delivered, technically solid, but emotionally sterile. A brilliant performance missing its soul. So, this time, I stepped out not just with choreography, but with conviction. I danced like my message depended on it because it did.

Not in a glittery routine. But in grounded presence—an invitation for the audience to join me. To feel something. To move their bodies in a space where that kind of thing "wasn't done."

And the response? It wasn't rejection. It was reverence.

People didn't check out. They lit up. They remembered. Not just the content—the experience.

It was Strategic Unruliness™ in motion—proof that resistance isn't a stop sign. It's a spark. A chance to move with, not against, what's true.

You'd think the most challenging part was getting clear. Saying the thing. Making the move.

It's not.

The real test comes after clarity—when the world starts testing how serious you are.

Because clarity changes your posture. Resistance tests your spine.

This isn't the quiet of the aftermath.
This is the pressure of pushback—from the world, from your wiring, from everything that says "Go back. Play small. Be reasonable."

Because this is what resistance looks like: You're doing something new. Unfamiliar. You're walking a road that hasn't been walked in your way. And when that happens, you get pushback. From others. From yourself.

You don't want to fail. Look foolish. Be rejected. Let people down. So, you retreat. Even when the thing you're retreating from is the very thing you were born to do.

Let's be clear: Resistance comes in two forms.
There's the internal kind—the doubt, the fear, the urge to stay small.
And there's the external kind—the voices telling you why it won't work, why it's too risky, why your way is wrong.

When I launched Project BE Confident—a program designed to build confidence in pre-teen and teenage girls—I called my dad, so proud I could burst.

I told him the vision. The mission. The model.

And his response?
"Who's going to pay for that?"
"Is that even a real need?"
"Why would you do that when you could be billing hours as a lawyer?"

My heart sank.

What if he's right?
What if this is stupid?
Who do I think I am?

Then the anger came—not just because he doubted me, but because I wanted him to believe so badly. It wasn't just disbelief. It was fear, cloaked in love, tangled in old rules—his, not mine.

But when the sting softened, I saw it:
That wasn't about me.
That was his fear. His wiring. His rules.

This is what other people's resistance looks like.
And if you mistake their fear for your truth, you'll abandon the very thing you're here to build.

Resistance doesn't mean stop.
It means to pay attention.
It means something important is happening.

Because the truth is, everything meaningful I've ever built came with resistance.
Every bold move I've made came with a voice—mine or someone else's—telling me not to.
And every time I moved through it?
It didn't just expand me.
It expanded what was possible for everyone watching.

But here's the part most people don't talk about:
Once you face the resistance—and move through it—you enter a different kind of discomfort.

Uncertainty.

Not the panic of doing something wrong.
The ache of not yet knowing what's right.

That's what happened when I ended a consulting relationship that was misaligned. They paid well—but asked for more than they were willing to give. Time. Access. Energy. And every time I overdelivered, I felt more depleted.

I finally ended it. Then came silence.

Three months. No new clients. No momentum. Just quiet.

The voice in my head screamed: "You totally messed up. You had something. Now you have nothing."

Even one of my closest friends said I was arrogant for walking away.

But it wasn't ego. It was integrity. It was alignment.

And after three months of clarity, discernment, and holding the line—the best client I've ever had walked through the door. Fully aligned. Full fee—and then some.

That only happened because I didn't flinch in the uncertainty.

And what held me through the silence wasn't a strategy.
It was conviction.

Not the loud kind.
The quiet kind—the kind that lives in your bones.

Conviction is what allows you to say no to what doesn't fit—like the day I danced again, even after the room once walked out. It reminded me: *Your boldest truth doesn't need permission. Just your full presence.*
It's what keeps you from grabbing the first thing that comes along, just because it's something.
It's what anchors you when no one is clapping.

You don't have to shout it from the rooftops.
You just have to hold it steady.

UNRULY CHALLENGE™
Face the Resistance

Think of a bold move you've already made. Something true. Brave. Aligned. Now ask yourself:

1. Where did the pushback show up?
2. What did it make you question about yourself?
3. What part of you is tempted to retreat, and what truth would you hold onto if you didn't?

Write it down. Look at it with clear eyes. You don't need to push through blindly—but you do need to know the difference between your truth and their fear.

UNRULY MOVE™
Trust the Truth—Even When the Resistance Is Loud

Let conviction be the part of you that doesn't flinch.

Interlude
BARE TOES, SHARP MIND

I had just won a massive result for a difficult client. His medical license had been revoked. I got it back. It was a huge deal.

I rode the elevator up, excited, heart still pounding. The partner's office was on the top floor. I waited in the hallway until she waved me in.

I delivered the news—sharp, clear, proud.
As I spoke, I noticed her eyes drifting downward. Again, and again.

And when I finished—expecting celebration, at the very least acknowledgment—she didn't say congratulations. She said, "You need to go home and change your shoes."

My navy pumps had open toes. Apparently, I was violating the firm's dress code.

I paused. Confused. Surely, she didn't hear me.

So, I asked, "Did you hear what I said about the result?"

She looked straight at me. "I heard you. Now, go change your shoes."

That was the moment I realized my success wasn't enough.
Not if it came in the wrong packaging.

You can save a man's career and still get penalized for your feet. Open-toe pumps were apparently more scandalous than a legal triumph—proof that in some places, polish matters more than power.

And what struck me hardest—it wasn't a man who shut me down. *It was a woman.* She could have been a mentor. A champion. A model of what it looks like to lift another woman in a winning moment.

Instead, she made me feel small.
Like, even at my best, I still wasn't enough.

It wasn't about shoes. It was about power.
Enforcing rules just because she could.

That was the moment I realized that even women who have made it are still afraid that there isn't enough room for all of us at the top. Break the rule. Lift as you rise.

And never shrink brilliance to fit someone else's standard.

CHAPTER THIRTEEN:

Live Unruly

Your laugh's louder.
Your breath's deeper.
The whole world feels different —
because you stopped holding back.

No more shrinking.
No more split.
Just you.
All of you.
Here.

He was twenty-two. The youngest marketing coordinator that the largest Lamborghini dealership in North Miami had ever hired. So young that they just called him "The Kid."

His job wasn't glamorous. He wasn't closing deals or test-driving supercars. He was behind the scenes—running social media, designing graphics, coordinating events, taping buyers' guides to windshields, and handing out water when the sales floor was slammed.

But that wasn't his edge.
His genius? *People.*

He made every customer feel like royalty. The special-needs teenager who came to sit in a Lamborghini on his birthday? The Kid made him feel like a rock star. The dad and son pulling up in a minivan? Greeted like VIPs—before The Kid even knew they owned one of the largest exotic car collections in North America.

It didn't matter who you were. If you walked through those doors, he made you feel like you belonged.

And people noticed. They came back just to talk to him. The energy shifted when he was around. Something about his presence made people lean in, exhale, and believe they belonged in a place like that, too.

But his boss didn't like it.

"I didn't hire you to be an entertainer," he said. "Get back to your job. Let the salespeople handle the customers."

So, he did. He shrank. Watched his words. Pulled back.

Until the day a man walked in and started circling the Pagani. Three million dollars. The most expensive car in the building. And no one greeted him.

No salespeople moved. So, The Kid did.

He started a conversation. Casual. Curious. Real. He could feel his boss watching. Feel the tension. The pull to back down. But he stayed.

Because this man wasn't browsing. He was buying.

So, The Kid made a call. To connect. To show up. To trust what he knew, even with someone breathing down his neck.

And the man bought the car. Not because of a pitch. Not because of a discount. Because of him. Because of how he showed up. Because of how he made the man feel.

He chose connection over compliance.
Presence over protocol.
And it paid off.

And what did he get for it? No commission. No credit. No thank you.
Just a lecture.

He was told he was out of line. That he didn't know his place.

He stood there—after closing the biggest sale of the year—being told he was wrong. And still, he didn't regret it because he knew what was right.

Brilliance doesn't ask for permission.
It doesn't wait to be invited.
And it rarely fits the mold.

You can't KPI your way to it. You can't forecast it or formula it or manage it into being.

You must make space for it. See it. Trust it. Let it lead.

Because brilliance doesn't always show up in the package you expect.

Sometimes it comes with tattoos or tears or a wild idea that makes the room go quiet. Sometimes it's emotional intelligence. Or deep intuition. Or the courage to say what everyone else is afraid to name. Sometimes it's the person who doesn't talk much in meetings but sends a late-night email that shifts the whole strategy. Sometimes it's the artist who sees what's possible before the data says it's real.

But most teams never unlock that kind of brilliance. Not because it isn't there. But because the culture isn't safe enough, brave enough, or spacious enough to let it out.

We keep people in the role they were hired to play. We keep leaders in the box we've seen before. We keep brilliance in a cage of compliance and then wonder why everyone feels stuck.

Because real capacity doesn't come from longer hours or tighter KPIs. It comes from aliveness. From knowing you're seen. From being allowed to give the full range of what you have.

According to the American Psychological Association, 93% of employees who feel valued are motivated to do their best work. And 88% feel more engaged.

This isn't warm and fuzzy.

It's the firepower behind your bottom line.

The Kid wasn't just doing his job. He was doing what he was made to do. He was bringing the full force of his presence, his intuition, his joy. And the moment that got shut down? The company didn't just lose morale. They lost millions.

That's what happens when we fail to unleash the brilliance on our teams. Not because people aren't capable—but because we haven't created a container where that brilliance is welcomed. Encouraged. Rewarded.

Unleashing brilliance isn't about asking people to do more. It's about allowing them to bring more of themselves.

And that's what the best leaders do.

They notice. They invite. They amplify what others might miss. They spot the spark—and protect it. They make sure the Kid on their team doesn't shrink. Or worse, quit. They help him shine.

When you do that? Everyone wins.

But this chapter isn't just about what's lost when brilliance is ignored. It's about what's possible when it's seen.

When leaders stop trying to fit everyone into neat little boxes and instead start asking: What is this person uniquely wired to give?

That's what one of my clients did. A CEO in the creative tech space. He doesn't measure his team by hours. He doesn't obsess over online presence. He's not tracking keystrokes or filling dashboards with artificial productivity.

He's watching energy.

If someone's off? Not performing? Not landing ideas like they usually do? He doesn't start with discipline. He starts with curiosity.

"What's up? You good? You need a break? Something off outside of work?"

And if they need a day—or a week—to recalibrate, they take it. No penalties. No performance reviews. Just space to return with their full self intact.

Because he knows capacity isn't built by extraction, it's built by expansion. You don't squeeze genius out of people.
You create the conditions where it pours out on its own.

That's how you triple revenue three years in a row—not by chasing hustle, but by protecting brilliance.

He treats his team like artists. Athletes. Humans.

And what he gets in return isn't just loyalty. It's greatness.

The kind of performance you can't mandate. The sort of ideas you can't extract through pressure. The type of culture you can't fake on a website.

And speaking of websites—let's talk about the opposite.

There was another client. A major organization. On paper? Dream workplace. On LinkedIn? Perfection. Their culture page sparkled with buzzwords. Empowerment. Innovation. Agility.

But when I went inside?

It was a graveyard of capacity.

Leaders cut out of the decisions. Micromanagement masking as accountability. Ideas shut down for being too bold, too fast, too "unvetted."

One executive told me, "We do weekly check-ins, but we're not allowed to bring new ideas unless we've pre-cleared them through two levels of approval. So now, we don't bring them."

Read that again.

Truthfully? This was the worst failing culture I've ever seen.

It wasn't just underperforming. It was optimized to avoid failure—and in doing so, it killed any chance at real flight.

That's the tradeoff most leaders don't see.

Safety can't come at the cost of soul.

And when you build a system that rewards compliance over creativity, you don't just lose innovation. You lose people.

Quietly. One by one. They disengage. They numb out. Or they leave—and the ones who stay? They give less and less of who they really are.

Not because they don't care.

Because they're tired of being unseen.

Here's the good news: That doesn't have to be the story.

You don't need to overhaul your entire organization overnight. But you do need to start asking better questions:

Who on my team is holding back—and why?
What gifts have I stopped seeing because they don't fit the job description?
Where am I managing output instead of inviting brilliance?

This is the real work of Strategic Unruliness™.

Want to unlock capacity? Start here:

- Where are your people playing it safe instead of playing full out?
- What ideas keep getting shut down too early—and by whom?
- What brilliance is hiding behind roles, titles, or performance reviews?
- Where do you feel resistance, and what's the rule behind it?

Not just expanding your own capacity—but creating the conditions where everyone's capacity can expand.

Want brilliance? Protect aliveness. Invite the whole person. Build for what's next.

And when that happens? You don't just hit goals. You unlock genius.

If any part of this is striking a chord—good. It means you see it. You feel it. That flash of recognition that this is the way forward.

Maybe you've already been leading this way. Quietly. Bravely. Sometimes without backup. Maybe you've held clarity in the chaos. Invited voices others overlooked. Chose integrity over performative leadership—even when no one clapped for it.

If that's true, then this chapter isn't here to persuade you—it's here to hold up a mirror and say, "See? You've known all along."

And if it's not true yet? That's okay. You're here. You're curious. You're paying attention.

Which means it's already starting.

You've already taken the first step—by feeling the pull, asking the questions, and staying open to more.

And when you lead like that—with conviction and trust and space for brilliance to rise—you don't just build a team. You build a movement.

One that says: *This is how we work now. This is what leadership looks like.*

And yeah—it takes guts. It takes clarity. It takes a fierce kind of love.

But you've got that. And we're just getting started.

Let's go.

UNRULY CHALLENGE™
Uncover the Hidden Brilliance

Think of your team—or your closest collaborators. Now ask:

1. Who am I underestimating, not because they lack talent, but because they lead differently than me?
2. What unseen brilliance is sitting just outside the bounds of our current structure?
3. Where could I pull back on control—and lean harder into trust?

Want to go further? Pick one person. Reach out. Ask:

1. "What's something you've been holding back here?"
2. "Where do you feel most alive at work?"
3. "What's one thing I could do differently to help you thrive?"

Then shut up. Listen. And follow through.

UNRULY MOVE™
Lead Brilliantly

Lead like brilliance is everywhere—and watch what happens when people believe it too.

Interlude
SMOKING ON THE ROOF

I hated that my mom smoked. One cigarette a day. Always in her bathroom. Always to unwind.

My sister and I were her personal anti-smoking brigade. Surgeon General warnings on the mirror. Sticky notes with skulls and crossbones. We guilted her hard.

What she didn't know? I was sneaking her cigarettes. And smoking them.

On the roof.

Whenever I was alone, I'd climb out, light up, and inhale like I had something to prove. It was the ultimate rebellion—secret, cinematic, ridiculous.

I never got caught. Well, until now.

That moment still makes me laugh. It wasn't strategy. It wasn't leadership. It was pure rebellion.

But rebellion has its place. It showed me how far I was willing to go to feel free.

Later, I'd learn that freedom isn't just breaking the rules. It's knowing which rules are worth breaking—and why.

Rebellion cracks the shell. Conviction is what steps through. And when it's strategic? That's when everything changes.

CHAPTER FOURTEEN:
Build What's Next

You've led from conviction—and now you can't unsee it. You've dismantled the noise. You've rewritten the story and reclaimed your place at the center of it. You've glimpsed what it feels like to lead unedited. And you're not going back.

This hasn't been about learning something new. It's been about remembering who you were before you shrank.

You've tasted what it's like to lead with your whole self. To stop hiding. To stop performing. To stop asking for permission.

And now? You can't un-feel it.

You might still doubt. You'll still hear the voices that say you're too much, not enough, off track. You'll still feel the pressure to go back to what's familiar.

But you won't. Because now you know what that will cost.

You know what it feels like to be fully present. To be heard not because you played it right, but because you said it real. To lead in a way that makes people not just listen but change.

You're not going back. Not because it's easy. But because it's yours.

You've crossed the threshold. You're not just thinking differently. You're leading from a new identity—one that doesn't shrink to fit, doesn't wait to be chosen, and doesn't outsource its clarity.

That's the shift. And once you make it, everything else moves.

This isn't rebellion for rebellion's sake. This is breaking the rules that never served you, so you can build what does.

It's not chaos or noise. It's not different for the sake of being different. It's clarity. On purpose. With guts.

It doesn't mean blowing everything up. It means you stop trying to win inside someone else's playbook.

You lead your way now. With Radical Clarity. With fire in your voice and softness where it counts.

You don't need to prove yourself. Or wait for the room to say yes. You've already said yes to yourself.

That's the pivot that changes everything.

Say it along with me:

They don't have to get it. I do.
Your rules do not define me.
If it costs my voice, it's too expensive.
I trust what I know, even when it scares me.
I'm not the right fit for the wrong rooms.

Because the world doesn't need more leaders who know the script. It needs leaders who know themselves.

The ones who walk in already grounded. Who hold nuance.
Challenge norms. Say the hard thing with love, and say it first.

They're not the loudest. They're the most aligned.

They're done outsourcing their power. They lead from the center. From truth.

And that path? It doesn't arrive fully built. You walk it, one brave step at a time.

I still feel it sometimes. Right before I walk on stage. The pull to shrink. To play it safe. To blend.

There was a moment—mic clipped, heels on, seconds from showtime—when I almost didn't do it. Not the talk. The opening. The invitation. The dance.

It felt like too much. But I looked down and thought, *whose idea of power am I still carrying?*

And I stepped out anyway. Because I wasn't there to impress. I was there to tell the truth.

Truth like this:

A CEO stuck trying to cut $1.5 million from a $9 million budget. One session of radical clarity, and we found the full savings. Not by slashing, but by sharpening. Cutting what didn't serve. Doubling down on what did.

A construction company whose exec team couldn't speak without conflict. But when we removed the noise? Communication became seamless. Profits jumped from 6% to 11%. Not from grinding harder—from finally working together.

A real estate founder, wildly successful and quietly bored. His team mirrored his disengagement. One session shifted everything. He stopped forcing a single track. Embraced the power of AND. Within a year, his new venture tripled revenue. Because he stopped following a blueprint and started building what was true.

That's what this work unlocks. Not just transformation. Liberation.

Even then, fear still knocks. That's when you reach for the reframes.
Not to erase the fear, but to move with it, fully intact.

Because fear isn't the problem. Stalling in the performance is.

And that's not you anymore.

These fears don't show up in a vacuum.
They're shaped by everything you've had to navigate just to take up space.

If you've been told your voice is too loud, your hair too wild, your name too hard to pronounce—these fears aren't imagined.
They're inherited. Reinforced. Sometimes, weaponized.

So, let's be clear. This isn't about pretending fear doesn't exist.
It's about refusing to let it set the rules.

Reframe the Fear

FEAR OF BEING "TOO MUCH" → They can find less.

FEAR OF FAILURE → Assume it'll suck. You'll survive. That's how you grow.

FEAR OF NOT BEING ENOUGH → You already have what you need. Nothing to prove.

FEAR OF REGRET → Inaction guarantees it. Risking it is the only way through.

FEAR OF REJECTION → It's not a verdict. It's redirection.

FEAR OF DISAPPROVAL → They don't live your life. You do.

FEAR OF LOOKING UNPROFESSIONAL → Unprofessional to whom? By what measure?

FEAR OF VISIBILITY → Hiding won't keep you safe. Just small.

FEAR OF DISCOMFORT → Change *is* uncomfortable. That's how you know it matters.

FEAR OF BREAKING THE MOLD → The mold was never made for you. Smash it.

FEAR OF TRUSTING YOURSELF → If you're wrong, you'll recover. Betray yourself, and the cost is deeper.

UNRULY MOVE™
Let Go of the Rules That Kept You Small and Build the Life That's Actually Yours

I got a call about a big event. Dream stage. Huge audience. I was excited.

But the conversation shifted. "Love your message, Kim. But I don't think our audience is ready. Can you water it down?"

A year ago, I might have said yes. Because even watered down, I believe in this work. But I'm not here to dilute truth.

So, I said no. Politely. Offered another speaker instead.

It wasn't just a no to that event. It was a yes to the stage I'm building. The one that doesn't require me to contort to be understood.

That's radical clarity in action.

If you're facing a moment like that—one asking you to shrink to stay—remember:

You didn't come this far to play small. You came to build what's next. Not just with belief. But with boundaries.

You don't need to fight to be taken seriously. You need to take yourself seriously enough to stop fighting.

When you are strategically unruly, you know: What's meant for you will never pass you by.

Say no to the limits. Challenge the old rules. Create the space.

And then?

Build.

FINAL UNRULY CHALLENGE™
Name It. Claim It. Build It.

Write down the truth you've been afraid to say out loud.

1. About your work.
2. Your leadership.
3. Your life.

That truth? It's not too much. It's your next move.

Say it. Stand in it. Start building from there. Because you were never too much. You were just too true for the old rules.

You've got this.
And I've got you.

Let what's true lead.
Your future is waiting.

You're not here to fit in. You're here to lead forward. And when you lead this way—with radical clarity, with unapologetic truth—you don't just build what's next for yourself.

You become the blueprint for the next generation of leaders.

Last thing, and this is important:
You're not alone.

You've got this.
And I've got you.

Your future is waiting.

ps. If you know your future is waiting, but you'd like some help stepping into it, I have the answer: www.strategicunruliness.com

pps. If you're ready to go change your life and this book helped you, would you help others find it too by leaving an honest review on Amazon or Goodreads? It would mean the world to me, and to them!

EPILOGUE:

So, What Now?

You've made it to the end, but you're not done.

This isn't the kind of book you read, highlight, and shelve.
This is the kind that lingers. That nudges. That *demands* a response.

Something opened in you while reading. You felt it. Maybe it was a crack. Maybe it was a flood. Either way, you don't walk away from that unchanged.

So, what now?

▶ IF YOU'RE JUST STARTING TO WAKE UP . . .

You don't need to burn it all down.
You just need to stop gaslighting yourself.

Sit down. Say the truth. On paper. In the mirror. To a friend who can hold it.

What's no longer working? What are you pretending you don't know?

Name it. Let it land. That's where power begins—not in bravado, but in brutal clarity.

■▶ IF YOU KNOW IT'S TIME TO SHIFT...

Pick one room where you've been contorting.

Then ask: *What would it look like to bring 10% more of me into this space?*

Not the safe version. The real one.

Say the thing you usually edit. Set the boundary you've been avoiding. Make the move you've been delaying.

Let it be messy. Let it be new. Let it be *you*.

■▶ IF YOU'RE READY TO BUILD WHAT'S NEXT...

You don't need more credentials, buy-in, or proof.

You need to start.

Make the call. Write the plan. Book the conversation. Lead the meeting with fire in your chest and clarity in your gut.

Not perfect. *True.*

Build the thing that's been whispering to you for years—the thing that's *yours*.

Not because you have all the answers.
But because you're finally asking the right questions.

▶ AND FOR EVERY SINGLE ONE OF YOU:

REMEMBER: RESISTANCE ALWAYS CREEPS IN RIGHT BEFORE YOU LEVEL UP.

It will sound like logic. Like timing. Like "maybe later."
It will wear the costume of wisdom, but it's fear in disguise.

Notice it. Name it. But don't stop.

You're not regressing, you're expanding. This is what the edge feels like.

So, when the resistance shows up?
Take note. And keep going.

▶ REPEAT THE WORK. RECLAIM YOUR POWER.

This is the moment to come back—again and again—to the four moves that change everything:

- **GET RADICALLY CLEAR.**
  Name what actually matters. Even when it's inconvenient.

- **FIND YOUR LIMITS.**
  Spot the invisible rules still shaping your decisions.

- **CHALLENGE THE RULES.**
  Break what no longer serves, with precision.

- **EXPAND CAPACITY.**
  Lead from the full force of who you are.

This isn't a one-time breakthrough. It's a rhythm. A practice. A way of moving through the world. And the next time it feels hard? Good.

That's how you know you're on to something real.

STRATEGIC UNRULINESS™
isn't a vibe. It's a commitment.

Not to chaos. Not to rebellion for rebellion's sake.
To *clarity*. To *truth*. To a version of leadership that actually feels like yours.

You don't need permission.
You just need to decide:

You're done shrinking.
You're done pretending.
You're ready to lead unruly.

And when you do—
You don't just change your work.
You change the rules of the room.

Because every time one person leads with truth instead of performance,
It makes it easier for someone else to do the same.

This isn't just your liberation.
Your freedom rewrites what's possible for the rest of us.

Let's go.

Afterword

Every ending is also a doorway.

If you're ready to step through, here's where we go next.

I've created a live space where I gather twice each month with leaders like you:

- To sharpen clarity until the next step is undeniable
- To break through the limits you didn't even realize were there
- To turn sparks of insight into bold, immediate action

This is the room where the book comes off the page and into your life. I'd love to see you there.

➡ STEP INTO THE ROOM AT WWW.STRATEGICUNRULINESS.COM

Love,
Kim

ABOUT THE AUTHOR

Kim Bolourtchi is a strategist, keynote speaker, and creator of *Strategic Unruliness*™—a leadership framework for bold visionaries ready to break limits and build what's next.

Before launching a global movement, Kim built a high-powered career as a litigator, leadership director at a top-15 law school, and professor of communication—all while secretly competing as a nationally ranked Latin dancer. She followed every rule and checked every box, convinced that's what success required, until the day her two worlds collided. In the middle of her biggest legal argument, she was outed to the justices of the Missouri Supreme Court as a dance champion. Minutes later, one of those justices found her in the courthouse bathroom, not to question her, but to ask how *she* could start dancing too.

That moment shattered the lie Kim had built her success on: that power comes from following the rules and checking all the boxes. It doesn't.

It comes from radical clarity, strategic rebellion, and the courage to lead from the full force of who you are.

Today, Kim works with global leaders, Fortune 500 teams, and entrepreneurial change-makers to dismantle outdated rules and unlock hidden capacity—not by doing more, but by removing what doesn't belong *and showing up with everything you've got.*

She lives between St. Louis and Miami with her husband and two labradoodles, and loves visiting her two amazing kids as they fashion their own unruly lives.

Learn more at www.kimbolourtchi.com or join Kim's live sessions at **www.strategicunruliness.com**

www.ingramcontent.com/pod-product-compliance
Lightning Source LLC
Chambersburg PA
CBHW071856160426
43209CB00005B/1074